Don't Be a Jerk Manager
The Down & Dirty Guide to Management
By James Monroe

**SECOND
RODEO**
— BOOKS —

ISBN 9798676944094

First paperback edition published 2020.

This book is dedicated to everyone who ever worked for me. I have no doubt they're wondering why the hell it took me so long to figure all this out. Thanks for your patience.

Foreword

In 2020, the global coronavirus pandemic brought unprecedented upheaval to the American workforce.

Overnight, many of us had to learn to work from home or take significant precautions at work. Over the first few weeks, thousands lost jobs. Over the next few months, many of us started to look at work differently.

The pandemic shocked us out of our routines and gave us a chance to see our work, jobs, and lives with a fresh perspective. The result was an exodus from jobs of all kinds.

Some people decided not to return to the workforce for personal reasons. Others changed companies or even professions.

As millions of people quit their jobs in the first half of 2021, employers scrambled. Signing bonuses, wage increases, and flexible work options suddenly became the norm at many companies.

And while all of that is good for employees, there is still a big elephant in the room, and neither bonuses nor pay increases will get rid of it: terrible managers, at all levels of American companies.

While it might be convenient to blame Covid-19 for all this turmoil, we must ask ourselves two questions:

1. Would someone who felt valued and respected, who did rewarding work and was recognized for their performance, who respected their manager, their co-workers, and their company, leave their job? A few might, for family or health reasons, but millions in just a few weeks?

2. Why has working from home become so attractive, even necessary? Is it just the commute? Or have many workplaces become so oppressive and toxic that employees dread going back?

The pandemic did not suddenly send millions of employees running for the door. Managers did. Bad managers have created and tolerated unpleasant company cultures over the course of decades. The pandemic simply put a spotlight on it and revealed options for those who were tired of suffering.

Employers had a chance to demonstrate compassion and flexibility. They were handed an unprecedented opportunity to support what they often call their greatest asset: their workforce.

Managers who did weren't coddling employees, they were maintaining productivity and retaining their best people. Managers who fell short did so in full view of current and prospective employees.

And perhaps for the first time, some leaders realized they have a problem. The problem, and therefore its solution, lies in the way we identify, hire, train, and evaluate managers.

When Gallup asked US managers what qualified them for their first management jobs, the top two responses were:

"I was successful in a previous, non-managerial role."
"I have a lot of experience and tenure in my company or field."

"I have management skills," isn't on this list.

According to the Gallup study, 82% of managers are not suited for their roles, and bad managers cost the US economy between $320 billion and $400 billion annually.

Miscast managers get frustrated. They become insecure and defensive. They lose focus on the business and they fail to take care of their teams. That's why so many managers–maybe even the majority–are jerks.

Being a jerk manager means letting your insecurities take over and allowing your ego to guide your decisions and behavior. It means putting yourself and your ambitions ahead of your responsibility to your company.

Jerk managers are weak and ineffective, and they are doomed to a career of anxiety, unhappiness and ultimately failure. But they're everywhere.

This book distills more than two decades of on-the-job management training into a simple, straightforward, practical guide. Its fundamental nature makes it useful to managers regardless of the ages of their employees or the cultural and economic makeup of their teams. It will help software managers, finance directors, and crew chiefs.

This isn't about setting the vision for a huge corporation, managing change or workplace psychology.

It's about how to excel in the trenches.

Table of Contents

Introduction

Are You a Jerk Manager?

If you manage people in a US company, the answer is likely to be, "Yes."

No matter how experienced you are, how much money you make or the title on your business card, it's likely that you have reported to jerk managers and have learned how to manage from jerk managers. And now, whether you know it or not, there's a very good chance that you–regardless of your age or gender–have become a jerk manager.

So, this book is for you. Particularly if you are early in your career, this book will help you avoid the mistakes that I and millions of managers like me have made.

This book is also for people who have jerk managers. If that's you, reading this will help you figure out what you're dealing with and understand that you are not the problem.

It should also be helpful to Human Resources folks as they think about their corporate culture and manager training materials.

But I've Taken Management Training

The biggest problem with management training is that in most cases there isn't any. There's plenty of training on topics like employment law, discrimination and insider trading, but rarely—if ever—do companies provide training on how to inspire and reward a team, communicate well, or manage a boss.

There's plenty of training for managers, but there's precious little training in management.

Most company-administered management training focuses on company policy and employment law because most training is designed to reduce the company's risk of lawsuits. That's incredibly important, and that kind of training will help keep you and your company out of legal trouble.

But it's not illegal to be a bad manager. You can follow every company policy and every employment law and still be a terrible manager.

You should absolutely embrace company training programs. These programs are usually very well done and can help you understand the letter and the spirit of employment laws and company policies. You won't find any of that in this book. This book is designed to make you a better manager so you get the most out of your team and grow your career.

Turn to other resources for legal and policy advice that is specific to your company, city, and state. You should have no problem finding them.

For Young Managers

You may think you have a pretty good idea of what it means to be a manager, but you're probably wrong.

Sure, you've had managers before and you've watched as they managed their teams and seen how they motivate employees. You've also seen the perks they enjoy and the magic of an expense account. But unless you've been very lucky, you've probably never been exposed to real management talent.

If you've had a great manager who took the time to mentor you, was open and trustworthy, who led by example and demonstrated excellent people skills (and if you were paying close attention) then you might be OK. But most managers, probably including most of the managers you've had, aren't very good at managing. And many are truly terrible.

Bad managers let their egos get in the way, they focus on the wrong things, they don't respect their teams, they attempt to motivate using fear and intimidation, they're insecure. If any of this sounds familiar, you've had bad managers and you've probably picked up a few bad habits.

But you're reading this, so you realize there's more to learn. You're already showing promise.

This book is the result of years of learning on the job, making lots of mistakes, being managed badly and being managed well, seeing how others manage and experiencing moments of real joy as a manager. It's intended to help you start your management career with the greatest possible chance of success—to evaluate jobs, companies, teams, and bosses, make good career choices, and thrive in your management career.

For Experienced Managers

As I've talked to other managers while writing this book, a consistent complaint has emerged: nobody ever taught any of us how to manage. There are a few exceptions–usually people who have been informally mentored by exceptional managers–but those are very rare.

Experienced managers may see themselves in this book. Maybe not in a flattering way, but that's OK. Reading this book will be the first step to becoming a better manager.

Be warned–it won't be easy. You will need to check your ego and strengthen your convictions. You will need to unlearn much of what you know, and you'll have to be willing to try new things that may be uncomfortable at first. But once you see how your team reacts, you'll discover how rewarding it can be to manage well.

Those rare managers who see their beliefs and behavior reflected here will realize they're not alone in the way they think about management. They may see opportunities to polish their skills, but mostly they may decide to mentor and inspire other managers, which is desperately needed.

For Managers Who Don't Like Managing

If you don't like managing people, it may be because you're doing it wrong. And honestly, that may not be your fault. Most managers are thrown into their roles with no help at all.

If management seems mysterious, your people seem difficult, and you just don't feel comfortable or successful as a manager, this book should help.

In fact, it may completely change the way you feel about your job. It may make you feel successful.

It's also possible you simply aren't cut out to manage people, and this book should help you figure that out too. There's no shame in deciding that management isn't for you, and it's better for everyone– particularly you–if you do.

For Anyone with a Bad Manager

If you work for a bad manager, this book will help you understand what's wrong and give you the language you need to address your manager's shortcomings. Depending on your manager, there may be a way to raise problems and suggest things they can do to improve.

Or you might just want to give your manager a copy of this book. Anonymously, of course.

You may also discover that it's best for you to find a new job. There are some situations that can be neither fixed nor tolerated, so this book may help you decide if you're trapped in one of those.

At the least, this book will help you realize you are not responsible for your bad boss. Very often there's nothing wrong with you, but like a battered child, you keep trying to improve only to discover that nothing changes. Realizing that it's your boss, not you, is pretty powerful and may make it easier for you to step away.

Part One: The Essentials

This section is about you, and the essential qualities you must have in order to be a great manager.

To successfully manage others, you first need to be able to manage your own character and ego. This will require you to take a good look at yourself and think as objectively as possible about how others see you.

For some people, this won't be easy. For many, it won't be possible. But if you can do it, you will be on your way to becoming a very successful manager.

Here are the essential things you need to do in order to be a good manager:

- Keep your ego in check
- Keep your focus on the business
- Communicate constantly and honestly
- Promote your team
- Admit your mistakes
- Don't be afraid to make hard decisions

These first few chapters will help you accomplish all of this.

Chapter 1: The Laws of Management

Let's start with a few concepts that you'll find to be true over and over. I call them The Laws of Management. These are a lot like laws of nature: they exist and there's nothing you can do about them. They will have a tremendous influence over your job and your career, so don't fight them. Understand them and put them to work for you.

The Laws of Management
1. Respect is earned, not granted
2. People are generally good
3. Everybody knows everything
4. You are not a genius
5. The person with the smallest ego wins

Let's take these one by one:

1. Respect is earned, not granted

You don't get to decide whether your people respect you. Your people will decide whether they respect you. It's not in your control.

Regardless of your title, your alma mater or the cost of your suit, you will get no respect until you earn it. A fancy title or impressive resume might elicit a little fear, but that's not even close to respect.

Respect comes from people who see that you're good at your job. It comes from team members who feel you understand their challenges, and who believe you are honest with them and are looking out for their well-being.

Respect comes from lots of exposure to you and seeing you demonstrate these qualities. You can't tell your team you have their backs; you have to show it. You can't tell them how experienced you are; they need to see the results of that experience with their own eyes. You can't say you'll always be honest; you simply must be honest consistently and over time.

And you can't ever trot out your title, resumé, or connection with the boss.

As soon as you hear yourself say, "I'm the Director of Whatever so what I say goes," you've failed. Worse, you've just said you can't explain why your decision is a good one, so you pulled rank. Jerk move. You've convinced no one that you are making the right decision, but you've shown everyone that you are an insecure weenie.

2. People are generally good

In every part of life, there is ample evidence this is true. Strangers hold doors for each other. Grocery store staff will help you find the coffee filters. People return lost purses and watch for Amber Alert cars and make faces at babies just to see them smile.

So why, in the workplace, do so many managers assume the worst?

Most employees are good people. Most want to help make the company successful. They want to do a good job and they want to work in a pleasant environment. They want to get along with their manager and their co-workers.

But so many managers think of their employees as ingrates who will try to get away with whatever they can. They believe–and sometimes say out loud–their employees are lucky to have jobs. They treat their people with suspicion and make rules to prevent abuse that wasn't likely to happen in the first place.

And when they do, they flush any goodwill they might have had down the toilet. Employees who feel they aren't trusted don't trust you. People who believe the company expects gratitude are reluctant to give it. Why should they? How does the company show its gratitude to them?

There are certainly sociopaths and narcissists in the world and most of them make it into the workforce. Those people are not generally good, but there aren't that many of them out there.

You'll be right more often than wrong if you start each interaction with the belief that your employees are good. More importantly, they'll believe that about you too.

And if it one turns out to be a sociopath after all, you'll know soon enough. You've lost nothing by assuming the best.

3. Everybody knows everything

It's human nature to talk. We're social animals, and we really don't have many boundaries. We'll tell a co-worker—in confidence of course—how much we make, what our score was on our last performance review, or that we've played golf with the boss.

And our co-worker will pass all that on, also in confidence, to someone else. In about ten minutes, everyone knows everything.

As a manager, realizing this and thinking about it often will keep you out of trouble.

Before you decide to give an employee a little salary bump or buy them a nice dinner, realize it's not going to be a secret. Even if they deserve the perk, word will get out. If that employee is recognized by their peers as a top performer, the extra dough might feel justified, and they'll feel like they can earn it too. But if the employee is an average performer who's particularly charming when you're in the room, it'll backfire on you.

Do what you need to do to motivate and reward your team members, but be careful and realize it will all be public. Don't motivate one employee while accidentally de-motivating all the others.

I once worked for a company going through a very contentious time. Many employees felt like they were getting a raw deal and tensions were high. Someone managed to get their hands on the weekly payroll from our accounting office and they mailed a copy to every employee's home. Every one of us saw how much everyone else made, right up to the top, and it was definitely not what most people considered fair. Those were interesting days.

One way or another, everybody knows everything, so act accordingly.

4. You are not a genius

Sorry, but no matter how smart you are, you're not solely responsible for your success.

You have been successful—so far—because of a combination of circumstances. You may have skills, but you also landed this job because of something else: a well-placed connection, a good reference, or simply because someone on the executive team was from your old neighborhood.

You may happen to be in a growing industry with lots of opportunities to succeed. There are times of rapid growth when it's almost impossible to fail. You win just by showing up. To outsiders, you look like a superstar. But really, you're just lucky.

Or you may be part of a new management team and the person who brought you on has decided you, and by extension they, are brilliant. That doesn't make it so.

Whatever they may be, remember that there are many factors to which you owe your success. Because the moment you start thinking you're a genius, your fall has begun. Arrogance has taken hold deep in your being, and it will prevent you from repeating your past successes. If you don't acknowledge the support that got you where you are, it's not going to help you get where you're going.

And—not surprisingly—one of your greatest sources of support is your team. They can choose to make you successful or not.

Share credit with your team. Promote individual team members. You're their manager, so you aren't competing with them. Their success is your success.

Everybody likes a manager who builds and supports strong teams. And in turn, your team will support you.

Remembering you're not a genius reminds you why your team is so important. It helps you focus on them and banish that ego monster that is never far away, always willing to take over if you let it. Which brings us to…

5. The person with the smallest ego wins

You know you've been successful when you hear your words coming out of someone else's mouth. No, you're not getting credit for those ideas. Yes, you may be the only one who remembers where they came from in the first place. But you just saw what a big impact you've had on your organization. Your words passed through who knows how many challenges, layers, egos…and now your idea has become real. It's part of the agenda. That's a big deal.

In one of my jobs, I used to say, "I can do anything I want to do in this company, as long as I don't also want the credit." If you keep your ego in check, you can be much more effective than if you grandstand and expect praise. When people see you focused on completing a project rather than getting credit for it, they trust you more. They believe you have the right priorities and you're motivated by helping the company, not yourself. They realize if the project is successful, they'll get some kudos too, which motivates them all the more.

Of course, even though you don't seek credit, people will notice. They'll know who was really responsible for getting things done. But the moment you expect gratitude, you cast doubt on your intentions and push other people's competitive buttons.

And if negotiation is a part of your job, a small ego will serve you very well. Negotiations can be contentious, and you won't take the bait when things get personal. You'll be able to keep your eye on the important issues and not sweat small stuff that may feel good but doesn't really move the business forward.

I've seen arrogant managers finish a negotiation thinking they'd killed it, and a few days later realize they got nothing but a skillfully stroked ego.

Chapter 2: What Does It Mean to Be a Jerk Manager?

> 76% of US respondents said they currently have or recently had a toxic boss.
>
> *Monster.com Poll*

Managers are supposed to be tough, right? You gotta crack the whip and make sure everyone knows who's in charge. Right?

Well, not really. Good managers are tough, but not in the way you might be thinking.

Good managers are not tough in the way bullies are tough. Good managers aren't abrupt or harsh. Good managers aren't insecure or arrogant or defensive. Good managers aren't jerks.

Good managers have tough characters. They need to function without much feedback, put their egos aside, and have difficult conversations. That requires inner toughness and resilience, and a willingness to take risks.

And people know who's in charge not because it's the toughest person in the room, but because it's the person they respect and will listen to. That may be their manager, or it may be someone else in the company, even one of their peers. When managers feel they need to remind everyone who's in charge, it's because they're probably not. They've failed to earn the respect of their team.

Being a jerk manager means letting your ego guide your decisions and behavior. It means putting yourself and your ambitions above your duty to your company. It means ignoring the golden rule. Being a jerk makes you look weak and it nearly always dooms you to a career of misery and failure.

As a manager, your obligation is clear: you are expected to build, maintain, and lead your team in a way that benefits the company as much as possible. To do that, you need to get to know your team members and understand how to motivate each of them. You need to earn their respect and their trust. You need to make sure each of your people has the tools they need to do their job. You need to pay attention, provide encouragement and support, and have tough conversations when necessary.

None of that is possible if you're a jerk.

Why not be a jerk?

First, it's bad for your reputation. Nobody likes working for a jerk and only bad managers like hiring them.

Everybody knows who the jerks are in any organization, so you're not fooling anyone. Jerk managers usually have troubled teams. Turnover can be high. Your reputation gets around.

Manage like a jerk and at some point, you're going to be treated like one. A good manager is going to see you for what you are and boot your butt out the door.

Second, being a jerk manager gets in the way of your primary job, which is to get the best performance out of your team.

Jerk managers have trouble retaining top talent, so often they're left with "B" players. Building a team of reluctant employees doing the minimum just to get by is pretty much the opposite of what managers are supposed to do.

As employees, we should feel good about what we do. We should feel engaged because we care about our jobs and our companies care about us. Companies that foster that kind of culture deserve our very best work, our innovation, and our loyalty.

And yet, bad managers who put their egos and ambitions first, who lead by intimidation, and who don't communicate well can't possibly create an engaging workplace culture. Thus, they're left with people who are willing to forego engagement and simply collect the paycheck.

Teams led by good managers are engaged. Engaged teams are more innovative and more efficient.

Make no mistake: in no way am I suggesting you be soft. Being a good manager does not mean letting your people get away with things or standing by quietly as they walk all over you. On the contrary, it means inspiring the team to be good workplace citizens and to treat you and each other with respect. As you'll see later in this book, not being a jerk manager means you need to make sure the quality of the team is high, and all its members deserve to be there. Very often that means making hard decisions, having tough conversations and being unpopular for a while.

Think about some of your past jobs, and what motivated you. Have you had a jerk boss? Of course you have. Did you go the extra mile for them? Did you offer suggestions to make things run more efficiently? Did you support them when they faced challenges of their own? Probably not.

If you've been fortunate enough to have a really good manager, think about the contrast. You felt valued and listened to. No topic was off-limits if you had an idea or suggestion to help the team. After all, you were on the front lines; you saw things your manager couldn't, and they respected that.

You also knew what was going on with the company, the industry and the team because your boss kept you in the loop, and you correctly believed you were a part of the company's success. Your boss let others know of your contributions and may have thanked you or the team publicly in a meeting or email.

Because your manager put their ego aside and focused on the team, you were inspired and motivated to contribute to the business in a way that you simply would not have been if your boss had been a jerk.

Teams with good managers have less turnover and greater productivity. People who are managed well tend to stay with the company longer. Even when the business is relatively static and opportunities for advancement are not plentiful, people will often stay with an organization in which they feel comfortable and rewarded.

Finally—and this should be obvious—it's better for your career when you're not a jerk. As a manager, you will be judged by how well your team performs. If you are a good manager with a productive team that speaks highly of your leadership, you benefit in a couple of important ways.

It's easier to recruit from within your company when word gets out that you are a good manager. Recruiting from within is one of the best ways to build a good team: you may have access to HR information about the applicant's track record and you can get a good idea from their current manager about how they would fit on your team. Your chances of getting a high-quality team player are pretty good.

But before anyone is going to seek you out or be willing to join your staff, you must have a reputation for being a good manager.

Besides recruiting, earning the respect of your team benefits your career directly.

Remember Law of Management #3: *Everybody Knows Everything.* People talk, and if your team members feel respected and believe they are being treated fairly, they will in turn respect you and say good things about you to their peers. Those comments always circulate within the company and they will get back to your boss.

Given the choice, your manager will prefer a happy, high-functioning team over one that is harboring resentment and anger. Lower turnover, less risk of HR actions or lawsuits, better reputation within the community, easier recruiting—these all result from having a successful, well-managed team.

If you have an innovative and efficient team, if your turnover is low, if your people are happy and aren't suing the company or filing complaints with HR—well, you look like a good manager. You're more likely to get additional responsibilities or a promotion or a bonus or recruited by the competition.

That's why you don't want to be a jerk manager.

Things Nobody Will Tell You
Warning Signs That You're a Jerk Manager

If you ever hear yourself saying any of these things, you are a jerk manager:

- Don't you know what my title is?
- Don't talk to me like that.
- You need to show some respect.
- Because I say so.
- Just do your job and let me worry about the big stuff.
- You're lucky to have this job.
- Do you know how many people would love to have your job?
- Do I need to remind you who's boss?
- That's above your pay grade.
- I don't have time for this.

Chapter 3: The Difference Between Love, Fear, and Respect

> "You can't please everyone and you can't make everyone like you."
>
> *Katie Couric, journalist*

If you've decided that you don't want to be a jerk manager, congratulations. Now it's time to think about what you *do* want to be.

If you want to be brave, there are hundreds of examples of brave characters in movies. If you want to be witty, there are lots of characters in literature offering inspiration.

But you want to be a great manager, and in this, you are largely on your own. There are few role models out there, so you will have to develop your management style based on your own personality, values, experiences, and character. This is hard but far from impossible, and it's one of the most rewarding things you'll do in your career.

Don't let popular culture be your guide. Movie and TV bosses are not good examples. They're characters serving a narrative, not people accountable for managing staff and delivering a product. Even stories about real people often simplify their managerial style, leaving you to believe they are "brilliant but demanding" or "relentless and visionary."

I've known managers who felt that being critical and harsh with their team made them look like Steve Jobs because they'd read that's how he managed. Of course, whatever his style, Jobs had a few other things going for him that these guys clearly lacked.

The better examples are real managers, good and bad. If you think back about managers you've had in the past, you may realize that the ones who weren't jerks had other issues. You may have had a manager who was eager to be liked but ineffective. Or you may have had managers who, while not jerks exactly, tried to project an image of toughness and relentlessness, though inside they were directionless and pliable.

Not being a jerk doesn't mean being loved, and it doesn't mean being feared. It means being respected.

Respect is not fear, and it is not love. Respect is the acknowledgment and appreciation of skill and professionalism.

And it's not handed to you just because you're a manager. You have to earn it.

If you focus too much on being liked, you're going to avoid making tough calls and having difficult conversations. You will need to do both of those things from time to time and everyone on your team knows it and expects it. In fact, team members are all too aware when someone on the team is underperforming, and they want something to be done, even though they'll probably never say so. They expect their manager to maintain high standards and weed out underperformers.

In your drive to be liked, you will avoid conflict, and morale and productivity will suffer. It will cost you respect because everyone will see that your priorities are in the wrong order. You're trying to be liked instead of respected, and ironically, you end up being neither.

If you go too far the other way and confuse respect with fear, you will look like a weak, ineffective manager. Nobody does their best work in an environment of fear and nobody respects a bully.

Managers who use intimidation appear insecure and shallow, like they don't really understand the business and are afraid of being challenged. These managers risk cutting off communication from their team members. After all, why bother going into the lion's den if you don't have to?

Managers who lead by intimidation diminish the image of the company in the eyes of its employees. Everyone hopes and expects their company will set high standards for its managers and will figure out when managers fail to live up to them. When bad managers are kept in place, employees believe–correctly–that the company doesn't care about them. Morale will suffer, and an us-versus-them mentality will set in.

Good news: the team will bond over their common enemy. Bad news: that's you.

Respect doesn't come with your title or your fancy office, it comes through repeated exposure to your team, letting them see that you are communicating well, making good decisions and supporting their work.

When your team sees that you don't play favorites or steal credit, and that you promote the team and its members to your boss and your peers, they will begin to respect you. When they see that you are fair, that you can make hard decisions, and are willing to admit your mistakes, they will respect you more. And along with respect will come trust.

I once had a boss who did all of those things. After working for her for just a few weeks, I realized I was in a very unusual but wonderful situation. Because I respected and trusted her, I felt free in every way–free to try new things, free to question the status quo, free to take crazy ideas to her because I knew she was going to treat me with respect even if she didn't support all my concepts.

When I promoted my team, she made a point of thanking my team members for their work, which made them feel great. They realized I had let her know about their accomplishments. She promoted me and my team to her bosses and we became known in the company for our innovation.

I'd rarely worked so hard or so smart because I'd rarely had the encouragement, inspiration and safety she provided. I felt nothing but respect for my boss, and I worked hard to earn hers.

I've also worked for someone who was overly nice. I remember that time in my career as a bit rudderless. I never knew whether I was on the right track or whether my boss was just too nice to guide me.

And I've worked for a bully. A couple of them actually. Screamers who liked to publicly humiliate, taunt and mock. While I did some good work in those jobs, I would say those were the least innovative periods of my career. Bully bosses make any deviation from the status quo feel risky. You never know what will trigger their insecurities, so people keep their heads down and try not to make waves. Innovation makes waves, so with a bully in charge, innovation suffers and the company ends up losing.

Lots of people feared these bully bosses, but nobody respected or trusted them.

Work to earn the respect of your team by being a great manager. Let them develop respect for your professionalism and managerial skills. Don't try to be their best friend and don't lead by intimidation.

Chapter 4: The Dangers of Success

As you climb your career ladder, as you work to keep your ego in check and your focus on your people and the job, you will confront an insidious new threat.

Success.

Success brings with it lots of potential pitfalls. It tricks you into believing things that aren't true. It changes the way others see you. It can change the way you see yourself. And unless you realize this, success can make you less successful.

As you become more successful, it can be harder to see what has made you that way. You may start thinking you're a different person, or in a different league than you used to be. Some of this is arrogance. Some of it is the belief that you need to change priorities as your responsibilities increase. All of it is bad.

People's expectations of you change as you become successful. You go from being a regular person to being a regular person *despite your success*. Sadly, people will have lower expectations of your humanity as you rise, and that may tempt you to live up to those lower standards.

When you're a coworker, you're just a decent person.

When you're a manager, you're a down-to-earth person despite being the boss.

When you're a senior executive, you're a big shot who's never too important to say, "Good morning," to the receptionist.

You're the same, but you're seen differently by others.

People expect you to become a jerk manager as you become more successful, so it's very important that you fight that impulse and prove them wrong. You're still one of the team, no matter what you think success is teaching you, and you must not become a jerk manager even though your ego will pull you in that direction.

To be sure, you'll have a different perspective on the job. You'll learn new things about the business and have new relationships and obligations. But none of that should prevent you from staying grounded and remembering that your success is built on the efforts of many others.

Remember Law of Management #4: *You Are Not a Genius*. As you become more successful, that law becomes more important.

Success has a way of fooling you into thinking you are infallible.

You may win awards. You'll get promotions and raises. People will tell you you're wonderful and you may start to think they're right.

The business may be doing great, and you might start believing it's due to your visionary leadership.

Don't get too impressed with yourself.

Your success is the result of your talent and hard work, yes, but also the work of your team, the good fortune of your company, business conditions well outside of your control and probably some good connections.

In other words, many factors contribute to your success, and only a few of them can be attributed to you.

Let's look at two specific situations in which managers might get pretty full of themselves, and what might result. I've been in both of these situations, as a manager and as someone being managed, and it's remarkable how consistently these play out.

Part of the New Team

Someone in management has decided they need to replace part or all of the team running this business unit, and you're one of the new managers. You've been sent in to fix things, so you get to stroll in and make changes to an ailing organization. This is a wonderful opportunity. You have the advantage of taking a fresh look at the company without the burden of legacy and tradition and making swift changes.

No matter what you do, you almost can't screw this up. The deck is firmly stacked in your favor.

When you're part of a new team, you're there because someone has decided a new team was necessary. And whoever made that decision will be eager to prove it was the right move. They will want to show the world that the new managers are better than the old ones and that the new team is discovering problems and solving them quickly.

They will make sure their new team looks like a good one, and that means making sure you look successful.

You really will be successful—it's not an illusion. With your fresh perspective, you'll spot problems that the old team couldn't see and correct them easily. You'll be able to make changes swiftly and you'll have the support of your boss and the company's upper management. They expect you to change things. That's why you're there.

When your performance is judged by someone rooting for you to win, even if it's for their own selfish reasons, you can't lose. Expect the new management team, including you, to be praised and rewarded (along with the person who put the new team in place).

None of this means you're a genius, it just means you're lucky. It won't last forever.

You've probably heard of the 90/10 rule—it takes 10% of your time to solve the first 90% of a problem, but it will take 90% of your time to solve that last 10%. This is as true in turning around a business or a team as it is with anything.

Pretty early on you'll have made all the simple changes to your organization, the euphoria will be gone, and you'll be staring at a tough to-do list with that last 10%.

Now you'll be judged just like any other manager—tougher maybe, since the person who sent in this new team also set high expectations throughout the company with all their praise.

If you've spent your time believing the memos and thinking you're a hotshot, and if you've been ungracious toward the staff you inherited, perhaps even hinting that they were doing things all wrong before you got here, you've got a tough road ahead.

Now you'll wish you had taken the time to get to know your organization and your people. You'll need your staff to help you solve the problems that remain and to chart a course for the post-euphoria future.

If you've been a jerk, they may decide it's more interesting to watch you fail than to help you succeed.

On the other hand, if you've done the hard work of getting to know your team and understanding the details of the business, this is when it will pay off. You'll have developed trust with your team members, who were probably pretty nervous when you arrived, and you'll have collaborated with them on the first 90%, so continuing to work together will come naturally to everyone.

By now, the newness will have worn off, your fresh perspective will have grown stale and you will no longer be able to blame the old team for the state of the business. But if you have built a solid team and created a positive, constructive culture, your team will be ready to roll up their sleeves and do what it takes to keep making progress and keep growing the business under your leadership.

Right Place, Right Time

Here's another scenario that happens frequently during times of growth. Imagine you're on the sales team of a company in a new, booming industry. Everyone wants your product and even though your bosses keep raising your sales targets, you are living in good times so you keep blowing right through them.

In fact, you've done so well that one day, you're promoted. Now you're running the sales team, and your numbers continue to look good. So good that within a couple of years, you're in charge of the entire business unit.

Even though you have no experience with marketing, distribution, supply chain, production, finance or HR, they now report to you, along with sales of course. But your performance continues to be judged on the numbers, and your numbers are strong. You get some nice perks and a bonus bigger than you ever thought you'd see.

You've got to be thinking pretty highly of yourself right about now—a meteoric rise, increasing responsibility and a business unit achieving record success. You must be a genius—just look at what the business is doing under your leadership and look at how your boss has rewarded you.

But when demand drops—it always does—it'll be up to you to keep the business growing. You'll need to cut costs, streamline processes, evaluate new vendors, improve production efficiency, even fire your old pals on the sales team who stopped performing as soon as the going got tough.

If you grew cocky and believed your innate talent was responsible for the business's success, shooting from the hip instead of doing your homework and learning how the business actually runs, you're in trouble. And your team knows it.

Your team knows they understand the business better than you do, and that you can't possibly run things without them. There's been a power shift, and they know it even if you're too self-absorbed to see it.

Worse, if you neglected to share credit with your team, which is common when managers start believing their own PR, the team probably doesn't feel too sympathetic toward you. And yet, you are now at their mercy. If they decide to help you out, you'll be very lucky indeed. If not, your days may be numbered.

On the other hand, if you realized all along you were not a genius but simply the beneficiary of some very good fortune, and you took the time to get to know your team and understand how their areas worked, you'll now have their respect. Even more so if you have publicly praised their work. They know you care enough to do your homework and you care about them, and they will be prepared to rally around you and get things done in this new, tougher era.

Your image as a capable manager and decent human being will grow, which helps you with your bosses and gets you your next promotion.

The moment you start thinking you're a genius, you're in trouble. Remember that and stay humble, connected, and generous.

Things Nobody Will Tell You
Keep Perks in Perspective

As you become successful, you may get an expense account, a reserved parking spot, a nice office, a fat bonus, a company phone, a car allowance...there are lots of ways companies reward managers.

However, do not make the mistake of thinking you are a good manager because of the perks you enjoy. It's dangerous when you see the trappings of success as evidence of it.

You are not a good manager because you fly business class.

You're not a good director because the studio picks you up in a limo.

You are not a good president because you have a big airplane.

People can be terrible at their jobs and still have all the trappings of success.

You may be an awful manager, but you have a car allowance anyway because your boss is a crappy manager too and doesn't realize you don't deserve it. Or, you can be an amazing manager but budget cuts mean flying coach.

Lousy directors still ride in limos.

I've known managers who look at their peers' perks the same way a four-year-old looks at how much juice everyone else is getting. How is that helping move the business forward?

That said, in some industries, perks are a sign of your place in the organization. If having an assistant or a club membership is standard for people at your level in your industry, that's what you should expect. If you don't, people on the outside may think you are not what you say you are.

And if you really want to impress people as you work your way up, let some of your perks go. Nothing says self-confidence like a VP showing up in a ten-year-old Jeep while more junior people fret over their Porsches.

Part Two: The Down & Dirty Guide to Management

"Your employees come first. And if you treat your employees right, guess what? Your customers come back, and that makes your shareholders happy. Start with employees and the rest follows from that."

Herb Kelleher, founder of Southwest Airlines

Management is simply the operation of a team to accomplish the company's goals as efficiently as possible. But as basic as that sounds, it takes insight, self-awareness, confidence, and empathy to be a good manager. In order to operate a team, you need to understand how to assemble the right team then get the best performance from each member. You need to understand what motivates each of the people who report to you so you can provide them with what they need to be successful.

Think about a typical day. Are you dealing with a constant barrage of people coming to you with problems or looking for guidance? Are you playing Whack-a-Mole as unforeseen complications come up and your team stands by helplessly? Are you spending your day answering probing questions from your boss and justifying your decisions? Are you correcting your new hires for making the same mistakes over and over? Do you feel like your team doesn't listen to you? Are you dealing with so many things that are out of your control you don't have time to do your job?

These are all signs that you are not a successful manager.

Bad managers can spend more time grappling with their self-inflicted problems and their poor decisions than they do managing their teams. Any job can seem hard when you spend your day covering up your mistakes and dealing with team members who know things aren't going well. This puts you in a reactive, defensive position, which makes it tough to look forward and focus on the team.

Not only does being a good manager mean building and running a strong team, but it also means being a strong member of the team you belong to–the management team. Being part of a management team requires cooperation and compromise. You'll need to have good relationships with your peers but it's also important to speak up and defend your position and your people when necessary and appropriate.

You will be expected to help solve business problems and work with your peers to develop and execute plans. This is one of the great pleasures of management—to think bigger than your usual role and come up with ideas that impact the broader business.

Decisions you make at the management team level may affect the team you manage. But as long as you have an honest and trusting relationship with your team members, you'll be able to work through any changes that are necessary.

Being a manager also means managing your boss. That can be one of the trickiest parts of your job, but it's essential for your team and your career.

All that said, most of the time your job is to keep your team running smoothly and efficiently, and that only gets really tough when managers let their destructive tendencies get in the way. These personal demons interfere with relationships, lead to bad decisions, result in poor hires and create problems that take huge amounts of time to solve.

This section, The Down & Dirty Guide to Management, will guide you through the evaluation of your team, your boss, your role and yourself. It will help you understand the kinds of personalities you are dealing with, and how to handle each of them. It will offer advice that might seem counterintuitive, but that comes from years of management experience and learning from lots of mistakes.

It will help you through all the things managers have to do: build and manage a team, hire and fire, communicate, manage your boss, work with your management peers, and work with your company's human resources support systems.

And it will reveal something that most people don't like to talk about, often because they haven't figured it out themselves: how to deal with difficult bosses and employees.

Hopefully, The Down & Dirty Guide will enable you, when combined with your own experience, intuition, and skills, to become a highly successful, highly regarded, and highly compensated manager.

Section 1: Evaluation

Whether you're approaching a new job or taking a fresh look at the job you have, it's important to step back for a little while and take an honest, objective look at yourself, your job, your boss and your team.

If you're beginning a new job, try to separate yourself from the excitement of the interview process and the prospect of starting fresh in a new role. If you've been in your current job for a while, try to pull your head out of the day-to-day and see yourself as others see you.

This section will help you think about your strengths and weaknesses. It will give you a framework to evaluate all the people who are important to your work life–those you work with and those you work for.

At the end of this process, you may arrive at some interesting conclusions. You may have a new appreciation for your boss, or some of your team members. You may decide you're in the wrong role. You may have some new tools you can use to deal with people and situations that have been challenging.

This process won't take long, but it will help immensely. And it will equip you with the skills you need to be successful, or embolden you to make a career change.

Chapter 5: Evaluating Yourself

> "To be able to lead others, a man must be willing to go forward alone."
>
> *President Harry Truman*

Let's assume that you know your industry and your company and that you have the qualifications your job requires. Your skills and experience and education all fit the job description—that's why you got this job in the first place.

But experience and education alone don't determine whether you can manage well. Let's see if you have the personal traits that will enable you to be a great manager, and if not, let's see if you can develop them.

Are you confident?

If so, good for you. Your confidence will enable you to hear feedback and suggestions—from multiple sources—and not take either personally. It will keep you from becoming defensive.

You will be able to communicate clearly and consistently. Your confidence will help your team feel you know what you're doing, and it will inspire trust.

The danger for you is becoming cocky or dismissive. Your people should see that you are confident in the company, the team, and its members, but at the same time, you must be approachable and open to ideas and input.

If you let arrogance creep in, it will have a damaging effect on the team. Arrogance will make you unapproachable. It will give your people the feeling that no matter what they have to say, you already know better. Your team members will be less interested in supporting you, and your arrogance will prevent you from noticing all the eye-rolling.

The most confident, smartest managers all know one very important thing: they know they don't know everything. They are eager to learn, and welcome learning and feedback no matter the source. They listen to their bosses and their employees, and as a result, they are constantly learning and improving.

If you have trouble with confidence and are plagued with insecurities and self-doubt, congratulations. It takes self-awareness and honesty to recognize that, so good for you.

Now, get over it.

Insecurity is the most toxic characteristic a manager can have. It steals your focus away from the job and turns it inward. It causes defensiveness, which shuts down learning, halts improvement and kills careers. I've watched over and over as insecurity and defensiveness have ruined far more careers than criminal or sexual misconduct.

You must be confident because management is most often a solo activity. You've heard the term "It's lonely at the top." It's even lonelier in the middle.

You may not get a lot of direction from your boss, yet you need to provide direction for your team.

You may not get much feedback or kudos yourself, but you need to provide both to your people.

That means you need to draw on your own strength, confidently chart a course and lead your team.

Unless your manager provides consistent guidance and feedback, and most managers won't, you will need to move forward based on your own convictions. You should be prepared to be on your own as you set your team's agenda and assign roles. You'll work with your management team peers, of course, making sure the entire organization is in sync, and you'll communicate with your boss, but your team's agenda and performance is on you. Nobody else will be blamed if things go south.

It takes strength and confidence to lead people. You need to be able to share credit with the team but shoulder failure alone. You need to promote your team's accomplishments, but not assign blame for their shortcomings. And if you're ever wrong, which you sometimes will be, you need to admit it and move on.

If all this sounds hard, management may not be for you. Seriously, be honest about this and re-think your career path. An insecure manager can harm morale and productivity and be a very disruptive force in a company. Insecure managers constantly avoid blame, dodge responsibility and claim to be victims.

Worse, insecure people are often effective bootlickers. When insecure managers are good at managing up, they can linger in organizations for a long time unless their bosses have the insight to understand the damage they're doing and the stomach to cut them loose. And when that finally happens, believe me, nobody will shed a tear.

Also, let's be honest. Insecurity is exhausting. All that worry, wondering about hidden meanings, looking for boogeymen. It's so much more productive to push all that internal crap out of the way and focus on the external things that make a difference, like the team and the business. But for truly insecure people, that's not easy to do.

If you struggle with insecurity, seriously consider whether management is right for you. If you decide to keep at it, do the hard work of keeping your insecurities in check and focusing on the important things.

Do you share credit?

Are you generous with credit? Good for you. Sharing credit for the team's success is one of the best ways to reward your employees and make them want to strive for more. It shows other managers that you're good at your job, and it helps you build a good reputation inside your company and industry.

Be sure to congratulate your team publicly, through emails or in meetings. When a team member has an exceptional victory, single them out. First, make sure you know your team well enough to anticipate the effect this will have on the other team members. Only mention individuals who are recognized as highly competent and avoid singling out brownnosers or credit thieves. Recognizing those people will hurt morale, as competent people see their peer's bad behavior rewarded.

It's understood in all of this that your boss will recognize what you're doing—being a good manager—and not think of you as a figurehead because your people are doing all the hard work. Read your boss to make sure they understand that when you promote the accomplishments of your team, you are also showing that the team is well-managed. There should be no question that this team and these individuals are performing so well because of your leadership; that should go without saying. So don't say it.

Does this sound like it will be hard for you? Does sharing credit run against your grain? After all, we go through most of our lives seeking approval and appreciation from parents, peers, and bosses, right?

This is one of the biggest adjustments new managers must make–realizing that your team's success is your success. As a manager, you'll get credit for making good hires, for having successful employees, and for managing a team that achieves group and individual goals.

You will not get credit for being good at the tasks your team members should be doing. If your team assembles widgets, your widget-assembling skills are irrelevant. It's your knowledge of the widget-assembly process and the way you manage your team that counts.

Good, confident, strong managers are gracious managers. When your team performs well, let them enjoy the credit. Taking personal credit for the accomplishments of the group–hitting a productivity target or reducing costs or winning awards–is not only unfair to the team members who did the hard work, but it makes you look small. Only insecure managers who are desperate for attention steal credit from their teams and peers.

Some managers are so credit-hungry that they compete with their teams. They want credit so badly that they will actually try to get it from their employees.

It can be interesting to think of the manager/employee relationship the same way you would think about a family. Parents are responsible for setting good examples for the children, and for inspiring them to be successful. That's what managers are supposed to do too. Can you imagine a parent showing how good they are at multiplication to gain the approval of their fourth grader? How pitiful is that?

Yet many managers are so credit-hungry, they seek approval in inappropriate places. If that describes you, you need to fix it. Just like learning to ride a bike or play the trombone, becoming a great manager takes time and effort, but it's possible to improve fairly quickly if you work at it.

Are you a good communicator?

Good communication is the oil that keeps your management machine running smoothly. Good managers communicate constantly with their teams about internal topics, external events, and industry issues. Consistent communication helps your team feel trusted and in the loop, and it gives them the business context they need to innovate and come up with fresh ideas of their own.

One on one, you'll want to consistently and honestly let your team members know how they are doing. Nobody should be surprised during a performance evaluation—they should have had several conversations with you during the year so they can make changes if necessary before the evaluation. Sometimes these are difficult conversations, but they must happen so your team members have the information they need to improve. Remember Law of Management #2: *People Are Generally Good,* so give them the feedback they need to be strong contributors to the team and the company.

Also, remember that you sit between your people and your company's upper management, so your job is to keep your team informed about what's going on in the company and the industry, and provide context that reflects the company's perspective. You should read trade publications and keep up with what's happening with other departments, but don't assume your people are doing the same. They're busy, and they're expecting you to let them know when interesting things happen.

If you're shy and communication does not come naturally, you need to sharpen your communication skills or you will never be a successful manager.

Communication gets easier over time. The more you speak in meetings and have open and honest one-on-one conversations with people, the easier it will get.

Everything in management takes practice, so keep working at it.

Chapter 6: Evaluating Your Boss

Only 19% of US respondents described their boss as a mentor, or someone they can learn from and they know has their back.

Monster.com Poll

Boss management is tricky, but it's a critically important part of being a manager. Proper boss management makes your job easier, helps your team succeed and keeps your career on track. But bosses vary, so consider the type of boss you have and make sure you're providing them with what they need from you.

All Bosses Are Human

Your boss is your boss because of an org chart, not because they possess special supernatural qualities. Your boss is still a person. Bosses don't have magical intuition that tells them what's happening with your team, so communication with your boss is essential. Don't make the mistake of thinking that your boss knows all and they don't want to hear from you, or that you're a bother when you go knocking on their door.

Like anyone, your boss has aspirations and ambitions and insecurities. Your boss also has a boss, and needs to manage up too, and there may be ways you can help with that.

Though bosses don't have all the answers, they often see things from a different perspective than you do, which may allow them to propose different solutions than you would.

And because bosses are human, there are all kinds out there. You will probably never have two bosses with the same management styles. Put another way, you will need to manage each of your bosses differently based on your evaluation of their personalities, strengths, shortcomings and needs.

Start evaluating your boss by looking at the six kinds of bosses you may encounter and learning ways of managing each of them to benefit your team and your career.

The Confident Boss

If your boss is truly confident (and not an insecure boss in a blustery disguise) this will be relatively easy. You can have open and direct conversations about what your team needs from your boss and what your boss needs from you. You can talk about how you can help them achieve their goals. And you can have a straightforward discussion about your team's goals and deliverables.

Confident bosses will not be threatened by open, honest communication.

If your boss has a good working knowledge of the business, including your area of responsibility, that's good. They can keep you on your toes, and you may learn quite a bit. If they're new to the industry, the confident boss won't have a problem trusting you to help them learn about your role and your part of the business.

The confident, secure boss will appreciate hearing about your team's successes and will want to know when individuals accomplish something exceptional. They'll be eager to compliment your team themselves.

The confident boss will value your communication skills. They will appreciate your confident demeanor and they will be honest with you about your performance.

The Insecure Boss

If you have an insecure boss your job is much harder, but at least you have plenty of company. I have had far more insecure bosses than confident ones.

Insecure bosses often have trouble with high-level conversations about the direction of the company. They don't like making decisions and they are slow to trust. They are petrified of making the wrong call, providing the wrong guidance and looking foolish in front of their bosses, so they often provide vague guidance or no guidance at all.

Insecure bosses are easily threatened. If your attempt to talk about your team's goals is met with comments like "It's not my problem if you don't know how to do your job," or—worse—all you get is silence, you're on your own.

Don't offer to help the insecure boss manage up. They'll think you're implying they're not capable of handling it on their own.

Instead, provide them with things they can use to help themselves look good, but don't acknowledge that's what you're doing.

I once had a boss who was so insecure, he hired a consultant to operate between him and his direct reports. I had a much stronger relationship with the outside consultant than I did with my own boss. It was just weird.

This is why you need to be strong and secure to be a manager. When faced with the insecure boss, it's up to you to move forward with your team, set your goals, coordinate with your management team peers, and use your best judgment, without much feedback from your boss.

Keep communicating with your boss frequently so they know what's going on and can jump in if they want to, but keep your expectations low that they will do much of anything to help guide your team or solve problems that may arise with your peers.

Deserved or not, be prepared to accept blame for things that go wrong, because the insecure boss will not. And don't expect much praise when things go well. The insecure boss will soak most of that up before it gets to you.

When you have an insecure boss, management can seem thankless, but don't let your team feel any of that. Be generous with your praise, find reasons to celebrate, shield your team from any effects of your boss's insecurities. And take a few minutes to acknowledge your own successes, even if it's only with family or friends.

The Bully Boss

The bully boss is the insecure boss but with fewer filters. bully bosses are so insecure, it's impossible to anticipate how they will behave, except you can expect them to be inappropriately aggressive most of the time. They are guided not by doing the right thing for the business but by self-protection and stamping out imagined threats.

Expect the bully boss to blame you for everything that goes wrong or that might go wrong. Expect to be ridiculed for the clothes you wear, the words you choose, and every decision you make. Expect a fair amount of yelling and to be berated for no reason—or at least for reasons that only exist in the terrified mind of the bully.

And unfortunately, expect your peers to stand by and watch it all happen. Nobody wants to be the next target, so bully bosses get away with their nasty behavior unchallenged.

Everyone working below these bosses will know they're bullies, including the people on your team, so make sure your people know you have their backs and you won't expose them to the bully's rage. And of course, never say anything unkind about the boss, no matter how horrible they are. Nothing good comes from that, and your team already knows everything they need to know.

Be careful about asking the bully boss for anything–for help or guidance or feedback or an opinion. They are too insecure to commit to an answer and may only perceive your questions as attacks.

In my experience, the only thing that can diffuse the bully boss, at least temporarily, is humor. Have a funny story ready to go and don't be afraid to whip it out preemptively when you see the bully boss approaching. Funny stories make you seem non-threatening and demand nothing frightening from the bully boss.

Perhaps you can find time to come up with funny stories in between doing your job and polishing your resume.

The Collaborator

Some bosses like to be part of the process. Particularly if their expertise and background are similar to yours, they may want to collaborate on strategy and tactics, and may want to offer advice at each step.

In extreme cases, this becomes micromanagement, which can be difficult to deal with. But often it's just a desire to stay involved, and it can result in a healthy exchange of ideas.

The good thing about having a collaborator for a boss is that you have someone with experience you can bounce ideas off, and because they are a part of the process, they have a stake in your success.

You will still need to set some boundaries: while you welcome collaboration, you don't want your boss to think you are needy or that you can't perform without their input, so be confident and secure through the process and maintain your independence. It may be better to say, "Here's what I'm thinking," as opposed to "What do you think?" That way you're looking for feedback on your plan, not asking for help coming up with one.

When you promote your team, the collaborator boss's experience in your field should enable them to appreciate your team's victories. But it's also possible the boss may feel a little competitive and might see your team's successes as less than their own. In this case, be sure your boss understands any unusual obstacles or challenges the team faced so it's easier to appreciate even minor wins.

The Hands-Off Boss

Many bosses don't want to contribute to the process, they want you to work with your peers on the management team to create and execute a strategy. Communicate with these bosses thoroughly, but treat them as clients, not as collaborators.

When you are working on a project—a budget, a five-year plan, your team's goals—don't invite them into the process, but create a presentation showing your plan and how you intend to execute. Imagine that you're a consultant or an outside agency. Present to them then give them an opportunity for input, but don't ask them to get into the weeds with you.

Work with your management team peers to make sure you have their support and even present together if that makes sense for the project. Most bosses like to see their team members working well together, so it will look good when you collaborate with your peers, and the extra input should make the plan better. Take your boss's feedback and return with a revised presentation to show that you incorporated it into your plan.

Some hands-off bosses are simply aloof. They don't communicate well—or at all—and they make it hard to know whether you're on the right track. These bosses can be very difficult to work for. They are often insecure and protect themselves by keeping their distance, so you don't get close enough to discover their flaws.

Try interacting with them in ways that don't require their feedback. Find opportunities to talk about work-related topics but keep it light. For example, when a competitor does something that makes news, talk to the boss and get their take on it.

If you can share some good news about your team, do that too. Don't ask for anything from your boss, make it clear that you're just keeping them informed, though you're always open to input.

Promote your team and your people as you would to any boss, but the hands-off boss requires some special attention. Watch them closely to make sure they understand your role in your team's success. They may think that you're lucky to have such great people and that maybe you're not so important.

That may be a little insight into how they see themselves, but obviously, it would not be good for your career. You can avoid giving the wrong impression by keeping consistent, open communication with your boss. Make sure you're developing your plans and setting your goals and hitting your milestones openly so your boss can see what you're doing. That way they should understand that the source of your team's success is your leadership, planning and execution.

The Micromanager

If your boss gets involved in the very small details of your job, and if they meddle in the day-to-day operation of your team, you are being micromanaged.

Micromanagement happens when managers forget to be managers and start competing with the people they manage. They need to show you how good they are at doing your job, even though they are often not very good at theirs. They constantly want to correct you, whether or not you need to be corrected. They confuse style with skill, so if you don't do even the smallest task exactly as they would, you're doing it all wrong.

Micromanagement is a problem with your boss, not with you. It's not a sign that you are doing something wrong, or that you haven't earned your boss' confidence. Micromanagers can't trust anyone to do the right thing because only they know what the right thing is. It's about them, not you, except that you need to deal with it. And it is unbelievably annoying.

I once had a boss who asked me to contact someone outside the company—someone I knew very well—then dictated the email he wanted me to send, word for word. Never mind that his email style was vastly, glaringly different from my own, or that we didn't even agree on what we were asking or what this person could accomplish for us. Never mind that I had known this person for years or that we had an honest and trusting relationship. My boss thought he knew better, and believed I needed his help writing an email to my friend. Now *that's* micromanagement.

(I sent my own email, by the way. My boss obviously had a problem, and I wasn't going to let him interfere with my professional relationships. Your network is one of your most valuable assets, as we'll discuss later, so tap it carefully and protect it vigorously.)

There are a few lost causes in corporate America—people who cannot be helped no matter how hard you try—and the micromanager is as close to a lost cause as I've ever seen. They will make your life miserable, hamper your ability to do your job and never be satisfied. If you find yourself working for a micromanager, it's time to freshen up the resume.

One more thought about boss management: regardless of the type of boss you have, never make the mistake of thinking that your boss cares about you personally or that if you look needy, they'll feel sorry for you and bail you out. Don't confide in them or ask them directly how you can have a better relationship. And do not tell your management team peers that you are working on your relationship with the boss. You never know what a political-minded peer might do with that information.

No boss–not even a great one–wants needy managers working for them, so always project a strong and confident attitude. This is yet another reason you need to be secure and resilient.

Chapter 7: Evaluating Your Team

Teams vary depending on the industry and the kind of work they perform. How you work with your team members will depend on their personalities, the way they've been treated in the past, and the company's attitude toward them.

But whether your team is made up of engineers or laborers, managing people is remarkably similar despite socio-economic or educational differences. Employees are all people, and they will respond to a manager who treats them with respect and has their best interest at heart.

Before you can provide each team member with what they need to be successful, you need to get an idea of who you are dealing with. Here are some of the types of people you'll likely encounter on your teams, and things you can do to help them excel at their jobs.

The Innovator

The innovator can be a great asset to your team. As long as you've established trust with your team and are an open and frequent communicator, the innovator will come to you often with ideas about how to improve things. The innovator can be the source of some truly great ideas, and they like thinking of themselves as going above and beyond to help the team and company. But if not managed properly, the innovator may become frustrated if their ideas are not adopted.

Manage the innovator by listening, by sincerely thanking them for the input, then follow up. If their ideas are usable, say so. If not, explain why not. If the innovator was off the mark, channel their creative thinking into areas that may be more helpful. Give them more context so they can think about actual business problems and brainstorm solutions. Then, if they have a breakthrough, promote them to your boss so they can have the satisfaction of getting credit for their work, which they will want and appreciate.

If the innovator believes you're not listening or that their ideas didn't get a fair hearing or a sincere vetting, they may go back to the team saying that you aren't smart enough or flexible enough or innovative enough to recognize the greatness of their ideas. That's a problem you don't need.

Give the innovator encouragement, a sincere hearing, honest feedback, appreciation and the information necessary to make strong contributions. Then give them the credit.

The Adversary

Long before you arrived on the scene, before they even knew your name, the adversary decided you were the enemy. This person has an us-vs-them mindset, and that may be fully justified based on unpleasant experiences with the company or with previous managers. Though you've done nothing to deserve it, you're branded the opposition simply by showing up to work. The adversary will treat you with suspicion and will be skeptical of everything you say.

And unfortunately, the adversary is often a vocal opinion leader, so their negative attitude may infect the rest of the team.

The adversary is usually the creation of bad managers. Managers who are distant and non-communicative, who are petty, who are credit hogs, who let their egos get in the way create adversaries everywhere they go. Companies that enact punitive policies because they distrust their employees create adversaries. Draconian rules about small things like office supplies, lunches that run five minutes too long, the amount of time employees spend in the bathroom—things that have nothing to do with the main business but feel harsh and punitive—just piss people off and make them feel distrusted.

If you are taking over a team that has had a bad manager, or if your company treats employees like bratty children, you will probably have an adversary on your team.

Dealing with the adversary will require confidence and persistence. There is nothing you can say to change the adversary's mind. You'll only make progress through your actions.

This is another example of how frequent, honest communication can work wonders. By being open and honest, by supporting your group (including the adversary) and by sharing credit for success, you'll show the adversary that they have misjudged you. Though they may never admit it, the rest of the team will see that the adversary is wrong to treat you like the enemy. You may not win them over, but you will defuse their attitude and blunt their influence on the rest of the team.

Whatever you do, don't treat the adversary like the opposition or single them out in any way. Doing so will only contribute to the us-vs-them atmosphere and show the rest of the team that the adversary is right. In fact, pay them a public compliment if possible. That will come as a surprise to people who expect you to treat the adversary as the enemy.

Through your actions and communication, you must demonstrate that you all share the common goal of doing great work in an engaging environment, and eventually, everyone will come to realize that there is no justification for an adversarial relationship.

This will take time, but it is possible to turn around a team that has been treated poorly by a predecessor.

Just keep your expectations realistic. It's unlikely the adversary will ever become a model employee. But remember, your goal is to be respected, not liked. Handled properly, the adversary should respect you and perform well, which is all you need.

The Thinker

The thinker is a methodical employee. Thinkers like to ponder a challenge before taking it on. They like to take their time and analyze things as much as possible. It often seems like they are doing nothing when, in fact, they would say they are very busy. They're thinking, not acting. To be honest, sometimes they are overthinking.

Sometimes the thinker gets so wrapped up in preparation, they wait too long to act. They may not structure their time appropriately, leaving too little time for action once all the thinking is done. Thinkers may have trouble with deadlines.

Thinkers may see their co-workers zooming ahead while they appear to be sitting still. It may frustrate them to see their reckless co-workers moving so quickly.

If you have a thinker who gets all their work done and does not miss deadlines, your job is simple. Accept their process and give them kudos when their work is good. Be aware that they may take some flak from their more active peers, but don't you make them feel bad for taking a different approach.

If your thinker is not performing as they should be, you need to have an honest conversation with them and let them know what they need to do to improve. Give them specific guidance, with a schedule if necessary, to allow them to go through their contemplations but get their work done on time as well.

Most of my thinkers were able to get on track and ended up being very successful. In only one case did things end badly for the thinker. And as nearly always happens, the rest of the team felt sorry for the person, but they were relieved that the problem had been solved.

The Favorite

As I'm sure you already know, some people are pleasers. They like to make other people happy, and they like to be thanked and rewarded when they do. In the workplace, a pleaser can take pleasing to a new level, and when they do, they become the favorite. Or, more accurately, they want to be *your* favorite.

The favorite thrives on showing you they are a little bit smarter and work a little bit harder than their co-workers, and they need your acknowledgment and appreciation for those qualities. They need to feel special.

In its mildest form, it's not so hard to manage the favorite. Give them pats on the back, thank them for going above and beyond. But don't tell them they're your favorite, even if they are. Remember, everyone knows everything, so once you tell one employee they are your favorite, everyone else knows they're not.

Give the favorite challenging projects. Let them stretch a little and show you (and themselves) what they can do. Just communicate honestly. Tell them when they do well and gently correct them when they need it.

The favorite can take things too far. They can take more of your time than they should as they repeatedly attempt to demonstrate their specialness. They can become discouraged if they don't feel appreciated enough, and "enough" can be a lot.

Worst case, the favorite may bypass you and start promoting their amazing qualities to others outside your team—your peers, your bosses, the CEO—whoever will listen. Once that happens, your problem has become someone else's. A member of your team is causing trouble for other groups or for your superiors, and the favorite is in jeopardy of becoming the fired.

I once had a favorite who decided to talk to my boss's boss about an issue he had no business discussing. The big boss, not knowing whether this guy had a point, went to my boss and asked him to look into it. Well, you can imagine how much my boss appreciated being given more work thanks to my employee. My problem employee became my boss's problem, which became my even bigger problem. It took quite an effort to save this guy's job.

The thing about favorites is that they are often very good performers. They should be some of the most successful employees on your team, but their need for outsized amounts of praise can actually put their jobs in jeopardy.

Usually, an honest conversation with the favorite will take care of things. Let them know that you genuinely appreciate their efforts, that you know they go above and beyond. The favorite should already know that you promote your people to your boss and your peers, but this is a good time for a reminder. If the favorite has gone too far, let them know that they have put you in an awkward position and make sure they know you don't want a repeat performance.

If the favorite really wants to please you, they'll get the message.

The Seller

It took me a few years to understand this fully, but there are some employees who really don't give a crap about pats on the back, a positive work environment, open communication or honest feedback.

These are the sellers, employees who live to close deals and collect commission checks.

Sellers are vital parts of any organization. Without good sellers, no company can be successful. And in my experience, the best sellers focus exclusively on two things: the close, and the money.

In fact, sellers are notorious for doing whatever it takes to close a deal even if it means promising more than the company can deliver.

I once had a very successful salesperson tell me his job was managing disappointment. He routinely sold more than he could deliver, thereby closing the deal, locking out his competitors and establishing a relationship with the client. Then he would gradually back out of the commitments he had made until the client agreed to accept the product he could deliver. They weren't always happy, but it was too late in the race to change horses.

I don't recommend this as a matter of routine–this guy had a charismatic and forgivable personality–but it's a good example of how the seller's desire to close a deal drove him to do some unconventional and uncomfortable things.

It's almost certain that rest of the team will not appreciate the seller. Sellers will be seen as over-promising manipulators with poor attention to detail. The rest of the team won't always realize how important the seller is to the success of the company, but they will see the mess that follows each time they close a deal.

Worse, the seller is rarely held accountable to the team. They move on quickly to the next conquest, leaving the team to handle the aftermath. As it should be. You want your sellers out selling, not dealing with internal strife, even if they caused it.

But somebody has to deal with the internal strife, and that somebody is you.

First, make sure the seller shows genuine gratitude to the team for their support. Words of thanks (and food) are good ways to soothe irritated coworkers.

Second, do your best to help your team deal with the seller. Listen to their complaints, show your concern, but don't sell out the seller. And don't set false expectations that the seller will improve. They won't.

Instead, engage the rest of the team to help prevent the chaos that follows in a seller's wake. Simple forms or procedures or systems may help to organize the seller, but they need to be very simple or the seller won't comply.

Designating a team member to work with the seller may make the rest of the team feel better. It gives them someone they can relate to and puts some space between the seller and the rest of the team.

And ultimately, talk it through. The team may only see the bad, so help everyone understand that the seller serves a necessary function, and the company would be in trouble without them, the same as with any member of the team.

The Butt Kisser

Remember that insecurity can be very destructive? The butt kisser is so insecure, they have decided they can't succeed on their own merits, so they need to hedge their bets by sucking up to you. And if you're not on your guard, the result can be bad for your image and corrosive to team morale.

The trouble is that the butt kisser is usually subtle. Compliments make you feel good even when they aren't genuine, so you will need to be extra vigilant to recognize when your rump is being romanced.

I've seen butt kissers of all ages, and I've seen them be successful with bosses of all ages and at all levels. Managers I really respect–seasoned executives–have fallen victim to skillful glute grazers.

Watching a 58-year-old butt kisser in action is bad enough, but seeing it work on a 63-year-old executive is sad and pathetic.

Truly, ass-kissing knows no limits.

The reason it's so important not to let the butt kisser be successful with you is that everyone else knows what they are up to, and the rest of the team hates it when they get away with it. They want to think you're too smart to be fooled by such shallow behavior, and they'll be disappointed if you are.

As a manager, you want to create a meritocracy, an environment in which people are rewarded based on their performance. The butt kisser attempts to bypass the meritocracy and fool you into rewarding them based on their charm, and you cannot let that happen.

Butt kissing can take many forms. It's not always an obvious comment about your haircut or your new shoes. Sometimes it's showing a little too much appreciation for your last email update, or laughing a little too long at your joke or passing on a compliment from someone else: "My mother says she really loves the changes you made to the product." Or one of my favorites: "Everyone says you're one of the best (or hardest-working or nicest…) managers in the company."

Some of their peers find butt kissers so abhorrent, they will go so far as to warn you about them. In my experience, it's very rare for an employee to come to you with a complaint about a peer. It's an unwritten law that team members stick together and let the boss figure out what's going on. But the butt kisser makes people so angry, they'll sometimes break that taboo and rat out the charmer.

When you hear one of your folks refer to "some people" or "one of the team" trying to "get by on personality," or something like that, you're being warned that the butt kisser is working you over. Pay attention and don't be a victim again.

Manage the butt kisser by avoiding any reaction when you see the kiss coming, particularly in front of other team members. Change the subject. In one-on-one conversations, keep the discussion focused on performance. Don't react to the flattery in any way.

Be consistent and the butt kisser will usually get the message.

But they probably won't stop trying.

The Defensive Player

This is a tough one. Defensive employees put up walls that prevent them from seeing things as they are and from hearing constructive feedback. They lack the ability to look objectively at themselves or their work.

When you say, "Let's get you some additional training to help you with this task," the defensive player hears, "The team has problems and it's all your fault." That's why their response often comes out of left field.

"How come you're not sending anyone else for training?"

"It's not my fault the task isn't getting done—my computer or my coworker or your management style is the problem."

You have a legitimate concern and are offering a supportive, constructive solution that will make them better at their job. You're not punishing them or doing anything that will hurt their career or reputation. And hopefully, you are compassionate and kind when you bring this subject up to show that you want the best for them.

But they won't see any of that. They can't.

Thus, you are left with very few options. You can keep trying to help them see the problem, but that's unlikely to work because their defensiveness blinds them. And while you keep trying, the job's not getting done and they're getting more and more frustrated.

They may quit. Their defensiveness may compel them to escape what they see as a rigged, unfair situation.

If they don't quit, you can put them on a performance improvement plan, spelling out specifically what they need to do in a specific timeframe. The shock of this may make them take another look at themselves, but don't count on it. It's as likely to intensify their feelings of unfairness.

Or you can start the process of managing them out (which should start with a performance improvement plan anyway).

Expect the defensive player to lash out at you. Because they can't see that you have a legitimate concern, don't be surprised if they go to HR to complain about you. The defensive player feels backed into a corner, no matter how supportive or benign your attempts to help them, so they defend themselves against these non-existent attacks by blaming you and becoming aggressive toward you.

Keep HR in the loop. Well before you have your first conversation with the defensive player, let HR know what you're doing so if things escalate (*when* they escalate, really), HR already has the backstory.

And set your expectations for improvement low.

Defensiveness is a complete career killer. In my experience, there's no saving the insecure, defensive employee.

The Doer

The doer is the ultimate task-oriented employee. They love to get going. They pride themselves on being fast and working hard. In fact, they usually think of themselves as faster and harder-working than their teammates.

The doer wants to get quick direction from you, then they're off. They don't want to hear about strategy, they just want to know what they need to do, and they want to know it now.

Doers are great when a project is broken down into tasks and it's time to start digging in. They will get annoyed by the prep, though. They don't always have the patience for planning, and they may make fun of the process.

You will be tempted to give the doer something just to keep them occupied until the project is ready for them. But be careful—the doer likes to do, but they also like to know that the things they do are useful. If you give a doer busy work or if you give them a task that they need to re-do once the project is more clearly defined, you'll frustrate them.

The doer likes pats on the back for being prompt and hard working. Depending on their maturity, they may know they are impatient and have a sense of humor about it.

Your job is relatively easy. Just channel the doer's energies so that they have something worthwhile to do, let them know they're appreciated and turn them loose.

Things Nobody Will Tell You
An Enemy in Your Camp

Any of these employee types might also be something I call the outdoer. The Outdoer is convinced they are smarter, better qualified, and more deserving.

Than you.

The Outdoer believes they should have your job. If you're new to your role, the Outdoer probably applied for it and believes they should have it. But since you're here now, the Outdoer will be on the attack from the start, looking for weaknesses, going behind your back, trying to turn your team against you, letting your boss know you were a bad hire, showing your peers why the Outdoer would have been a better choice.

The Outdoer must go. There's no saving them, and the longer you wait, the more damage they will do.

Don't think of the Outdoer as disloyal. Loyalty, like respect, is earned. This isn't about loyalty. This is something else. This is about not having the opportunity to do your job because someone is getting in the way. The Outdoer is working against you and the company.

You shouldn't fire someone because they are not loyal. Usually, it's your fault for not earning an employee's loyalty. But you can fire the Outdoer for being destructive and for not having the company's best interests at heart. And you should. The company hired you to lead this team, and by undermining you, the Outdoer is thwarting the company's efforts.

Not everyone who applies for the job you end up getting will be an Outdoer. As long as you have open and honest conversations with your team and you maintain good communication with your boss and your management team peers, you'll know when you have an Outdoer on your team.

And once you know, you need to take care of it.

Chapter 8: Leaders and Troublemakers

"A boss has the title, a leader has the people."
Simon Sinek, author and speaker

Every team has natural leaders, but they're not necessarily your allies. They can work with you or against you, depending on how you choose to manage them.

Many teams also have troublemakers, but they don't have to be your enemies. They can have a corrosive effect on the team or, sometimes, you can turn them around, depending on how you choose to manage them.

The tricky part can be telling them apart. Leaders and troublemakers have a lot in common. After all, you can't be an effective troublemaker unless you're also a leader.

If you don't manage a leader properly, they'll lead the team against you. If they don't have an honest relationship with you and understand the context of a decision, they may assume the worst. Their opinions matter, so if they think you've made a bad call or the company has taken a wrong turn, they'll be vocal about it and people will listen. Particularly if the company or previous managers have made a bad impression, the leader may decide you too have screwed up, and the team will follow suit.

You don't need this kind of influencer on your team, so don't let your leader become one.

Managing your leaders and troublemakers takes objectivity and patience. You need to communicate openly and you must not become defensive. You must put your ego aside and your employees first, even the difficult ones. Jerk managers can't do either of those things, so they end up turning their leaders against them and proving their troublemakers right.

But it's completely within your power to prevent that.

Start by identifying your leaders. If you're new to the team, you can spot them pretty quickly in meetings, or they may be the first ones to come chat with you and let you know their views of the team and the company.

If you've been around for a while, you already know who your leaders are. They're the ones other people glance at in meetings to see their reactions and the ones who will speak for the group.

Then listen to them while remembering Laws of Management #2: *People Are Generally Good,* and #3 *Everybody Knows Everything.*

Ask your leader what they think about the company, the product, or the industry. Ask what they would improve about the company or the product. Ask how they feel about their role, and what they'd like to see happen that would make them more satisfied at work.

You will quickly know whether your leader is a troublemaker or not.

If not, think about what you can do to capitalize on your leader's good qualities and reduce the effect of the bad ones. Can you give them side projects that will help you and challenge them? Can you put them on a management track in the company, and would they welcome that? Just be sure anything you say or do will be received the right way by the rest of the team when they find out, which of course they will.

Your goal is to turn your leaders into junior partners, to nurture their natural abilities so that they move the company forward. They are opinion leaders, so their views of you as a manager and the company should be important to you. Make sure they understand why you and the company make the decisions you make. Give them and the rest of the team context and let them know how the decisions you make are compatible with the company's strategies.

Your leaders are not your equals—you are still responsible for leading the group—but they can help by supporting your viewpoint in full view of the rest of the team, the people who are always looking to see what they think.

Don't try to con them. They'll see that a mile off. If they ask a question that you can't answer, admit that. And encourage them to come to you often with their questions or input.

Remember you are not trying to be their friend. You want to be professional and supportive, which, over time, will earn their respect.

If your leaders show interest in becoming mangers themselves, work with HR to put them on a management track. Two good things come from this: the more they learn about management, the more sympathetic they'll become toward your position, and they'll be forever grateful that you gave them the opportunity. In both cases, they will spread the word about your skills and integrity. And they'll think you're a pretty good judge of character.

By the way, when one of your team members moves up in the company, congratulations to you. You now look like a fantastic manager. You've identified and nurtured talent and you've made it easy for the company to fill a management job with a great employee. Everyone likes hiring from within.

Just make sure your protégé doesn't become a jerk manager. With you as a role model, that should be easy.

Dealing with Troublemakers

Oddly, you manage leaders and troublemakers in similar ways. In both cases, they have the potential to do significant damage, so managing them the right way will make your life that much easier.

Follow the same process with troublemakers that you follow with leaders: meet with them, ask them questions about the company, the product and their roles, and really listen.

Then let them know how you see your role, that you are there to make the team as good as it can be, that you will support each member of the team so they are successful and rewarded.

Remembering that people are generally good, assume the person in front of you has had unpleasant experiences in the past, perhaps with your predecessor, your company or some other job. Give them the chance to realize that you are different and the time to see you demonstrate it.

Not all troublemakers will turn around when they realize you're not as bad as they thought, but some will.

Whatever you do, don't react to the things the troublemaker says or does. Though it can be hard when people get aggressive or emotional, resist the urge to pull rank or accuse the troublemaker of insubordination. You need to keep your ego in check and not be offended, no matter how offensive the troublemaker is. The moment you lose it, you and the troublemaker are on the same level. You've let your ego get in the way and you've become a jerk manager.

There's another important reason to keep your ego in check. Staying professional gives you a superpower. It enables you to deploy the most successful tactic there is when dealing with a troublemaker at any level: have good, honest relationships with everyone else.

Troublemakers may have a hard time coming to terms with the fact that you're not like their other bosses. In many cases, their workplace persona is defined by opposition to "the man," so don't expect them to start your fan club just because you're not a jerk manager.

But as their coworkers start to see by your actions that you're supportive, open and honest and that your ego is in check, the troublemaker will become isolated. Their complaints against management will look like the immature rantings of a malcontent.

It's OK to rail against the man when everyone can see the boss is a jerk manager. But when the person in the manager's office is a decent human being looking out for the team, the troublemaker goes from being a champion of the people to an out-of-touch crybaby.

How the troublemaker will react to this new development is hard to predict. Depending on the frailty of their ego, they may turn into a good team player, they may remain distant but dial back the hostility, or they may start looking for other work.

In any case, you'll have done your best to turn a troubled employee around. And by keeping things professional and not reacting personally to the troublemaker's attitude, you show the rest of the team that you're a mature adult, you don't take things personally, and you're a competent manager.

Chapter 9: Evaluating a New Job

Whether you're new to management or have been around a while, starting a new job is always fun. You get a chance to make a good first impression and you get to establish fresh relationships. You will never again have as much influence over the way your team feels about you and the company as you have in your first few days.

But you need to think carefully about how to make a good impression and you need to do some homework. This chapter covers some of the things you should think about before you walk in the door on your first day.

Your Predecessor, The Beloved

Are you taking over a team that has just lost a beloved leader? Will you arrive at your office to discover some very big shoes under the desk? If so, show respect for your predecessor, admit that things will be different but let people know you will attempt to earn the same level of respect the team felt for their old boss. Then move on.

Don't focus on what the previous manager did or ask questions about how things used to be. Let people talk about the old boss if they want to, but don't you dwell on any of that. You're your own person and you will chart your own course.

Remember that the team's admiration for your predecessor has nothing to do with you. Don't feel insulted or try to compete with them or mimic their style. You have your own personality, style and values, so as long as you're not a jerk manager, you will earn the respect of this new team quickly enough.

You may even learn that the old manager, though beloved, wasn't perfect after all. Who is?

Your Predecessor, The Jerk Manager

Are you replacing someone who was hated, feared, or disrespected? This is a great opportunity to show that you are different, but be prepared for it to take some time. Based on their previous experience, folks on your team may expect the worst. If your predecessor was a jerk manager, your team will expect you to be the same. They may be slow to trust because it will take a while for them to see that things are different.

They may not trust the company either, particularly if the old boss left because of a promotion. That's a particularly nasty situation. Not only did the company do nothing to limit the damage to the team while the jerk manager was in charge, but the jerk manager was also able to trade on the team's good work and get promoted.

You can see how infuriating that would be. Of course, you can say nothing about any of it.

You will earn your team's trust and respect over time by not being a jerk manager—by communicating, by sharing credit, by putting your ego aside, and encouraging a trusting, open relationship.

Be fair and consistent, don't play favorites, don't punish employees who are skeptical of you, don't let the butt kissers succeed.

You may have a bit of an uphill battle on your hands improving the image of the company, but that too will come with time and with repeated exposure to you as you do the right things.

Of course, never criticize your predecessor. Even though your people—once they start trusting you—might delight in talking about them, it makes you look arrogant and a little petty when you join in and compare yourself to them.

Nothing speaks louder than your actions, so keep your words to a minimum.

Making a Good First Impression

First impressions are obviously important, but don't psych yourself out. You may be a little nervous, but so is the team you're about to lead. You're all going to get through these first few days together and it'll be just fine as long as you start off on the right foot.

First, take a quick look at social media, including LinkedIn, and see what you can discover about your team. Not everyone is savvy about posting, particularly to Facebook, so don't worry too much about what you see. At this point, you're just looking for some basic background information.

Then, on your first day, introduce yourself to everyone on your team. If you can, talk to each of them individually. Make eye contact and really try hard to remember everyone's name.

If it's not possible to talk to each person individually in the first couple of days, get everyone together as a group. You may need more than one group meeting, particularly if your team works in shifts and not everyone can get together at the same time, or if your team is spread out across time zones or continents.

This first meeting is for you to share some information about your background, talk about why you're excited to be in this role and show that you have an optimistic, positive view of the future.

Don't boast about your personal accomplishments, but rather talk about how you were part of successful teams. Make it clear that you believe the teams—not you alone nor your skillful leadership—were responsible for each success.

Tell people what you learned in your previous jobs. Then ask questions, listen and observe. Ask about the workplace culture, the product, the company. Ask people what they'd like to change about the team or the company, and what they'd like to preserve. Don't expect people to be completely honest in a group meeting. See who speaks up, find out who the opinion leaders are. Watch for eye-rolling and arm crossing and eye-contact avoiding and all the other unspoken communication that will help you figure out the team dynamics.

Then you really need to meet with each person one-on-one as soon as possible. When it's just the two of you, people will feel much more comfortable talking about the team and asking questions.

Start by asking each person about their role, their professional aspirations, their feelings about the team and the product. Don't ask about personal details, but take note if they are offered. Sometimes talking about children, schools or spouses is a way of laying the groundwork for future conversations about salary or time off.

Your goal here is the same as in the group meeting—share professional details, talk about why you're excited and show that you're optimistic about the future—except you will do a lot more listening.

And you may be amazed at what you hear.

I've had people tell me some crazy things in our first one-on-one conversations. People have admitted they don't like their jobs, that they plan to leave the company, that they are in the wrong career. People have spoken derisively about their peers and the company.

I've heard people openly express skepticism that I will be able to fix what they see as a broken team. I've had people tell me they thought they should have got my job instead of me.

People have expressed sympathy for me because they believe I'm in for a rough ride, that it doesn't matter what I do because they've seen it all before and nothing's going to change.

Of course, don't get defensive, and no matter what you hear about your predecessor, avoid the very understandable urge to talk about what they did wrong or offer why you're different. No matter how bad a manager was, they will probably still have an ally or two on your team, and there's no need to stir up ill will with anyone.

You will quickly get a pretty good idea of the employee types you're dealing with.

And you're being tested. Your new team is watching for your reaction as much as you're watching for theirs. Not everything you hear will be true and many of the opinions expressed will be exaggerated. But you'll never have another conversation like this one once you're established in your job, so pay close attention to what you hear.

Remember these conversations, but don't overreact. Take a little time to see how people work together and how they perform. Issues that sounded huge in individual meetings might not really be that important. Or just the opposite—things that seemed small may end up being big problems. That's why you don't want to react too soon. You need to understand the team better and figure out the context of the comments you heard.

(The only time you'll want to react quickly is if you encounter an Outdoer. If you have one of those, keep an eye out for deceptive behavior and start thinking about how you're going to get rid of them.)

In both group and individual meetings, don't make broad statements about how you intend to manage the team. It's way too early, and your people will believe what they see, not what you tell them.

Don't make broad statements about yourself either. Don't say, "I'm an open person" or, "I'm collaborative," or, "I believe in good communication."

Hopefully, these things are true, but there's something about hearing them that makes people doubt it. If you're such an open person, they'll discover that soon enough.

When someone tells me they're a good communicator, all I hear is "I want to be thought of as a good communicator, possibly because I'm not." I won't believe it until I've seen it for myself.

If people ask about your management style, simply say that you'll work to make everyone on the team successful and to make sure you all have a pleasant work environment.

Be confident but be humble.

Get to know everyone who reports to you, and if you are managing managers, get to know as many of their team members as you can. As long as you're not a jerk, giving people a chance to know you will be very helpful in building trust and instilling confidence in your leadership.

This trust and confidence will also make them feel safe talking to you, eventually allowing them to provide you with helpful feedback.

Honest and open communication, beginning with the first contact you have, will help build your reputation as a good manager inside the company, which will help you with recruiting and retention and might even get you promoted.

And when the time comes that you have to deliver bad news, your team is more likely to take it well because it's coming from someone they trust.

Section 2: Optimizing the Team

> "The function of leadership is to produce more leaders, not more followers."
>
> *Ralph Nader, activist and consumer advocate*

Once you've met your team and had a little time to see their strengths and styles, it's time to decide if you need to make any changes to the way the team operates. Maybe the team functions very well as it is. The right people are in the right roles, the team is efficient and the work they put out is good.

Or maybe the team needs some help. Maybe not everyone is a strong contributor, or a few unhappy employees are dragging down the rest of the team. Maybe they could be more efficient, or maybe the work environment could be improved.

It's your job to optimize the team, to make sure you have a good group working well together and consistently putting out a good product.

When they start with a new team, some managers believe they need to put their stamp on it. They feel they need to send a message that there's a new sheriff in town. These managers will make changes just to show they can, or to show how their predecessor screwed up.

If you inherit a strong, high-performing team, this will be a disaster. A strong team hopes their new manager will be smart enough to see how well things are going. When the team sees changes for the sake of change, they lose confidence in the new boss immediately.

And because these new bosses just want to show they're in charge, they'll often make changes when they first walk in the door before they really understand how the team functions. Then, not only are they useless changes, they are also mistakes. What a horrible way to start a new job–as a manager the team distrusts and who made a mess of things.

So be thoughtful and take time to evaluate things before making any changes, then make them with the input of your team.

Chapter 10: Fix or Fire?

Take a clear, objective look at the way each team member works. Are the right people doing the right jobs? Is everyone performing at about the same level? Is that high enough? Do their skills complement each other? Or is there a clear difference in the work output of some team members?

Optimizing the team—making sure each team member deserves to be there and they work efficiently together—means identifying your underperformers, working to improve them or moving them out.

This sounds harsh, but one of the most destructive things you can do is to allow an underperformer to linger on a team of high achievers. Successful people want to work with people of the same caliber. They appreciate meritocracy and want everyone to earn the right to be there, just as they have.

When underperformers linger on the team, drawing a similar salary and getting similar benefits, it's unfair to your strongest people. The last thing you want to do is de-motivate your top performers, but that's what happens when you keep poor performers around.

Once you've identified a low performer, your first task is to see if you can help them improve. Often, low performers realize they are not working to the same standard as the rest of the team, and in many cases, it bothers them. Even though they know there's something wrong, they may not know how to fix it. They may be afraid of asking for help, like training or mentoring, because it will put a spotlight on their poor performance. Though they will be worried that you've discovered they are not up to par, they may welcome your input and the opportunity to improve.

Sometimes low performers are victims of the team's own dynamics. I once took over a group that had several high achievers and one employee who was largely disregarded. She was considered to be relatively unskilled, and so was given mostly menial tasks. This employee was quite a bit older than the rest of the team, so unfortunately her age may have led people to assume she was incapable of functioning at the same level as the team's younger members.

In retrospect, it's clear that because she received less challenging work, she never had a chance to show what she could do. That sapped her confidence, and she stopped trying for more challenging assignments, which just confirmed everyone's beliefs.

As part of my evaluation of the team, I gave her the same kinds of assignments the others routinely received, and I was pleasantly surprised. With only a little bit of coaching, she came back with work that was every bit as good as the work the rest of the team was turning out. All she needed was to be taken seriously and given an opportunity, and she became a high achiever in a matter of weeks.

She had been sidelined for so long, nobody—including my boss—thought she had much to offer. But by giving her a chance, then promoting her work to my boss and my peers on the management team, I could improve the output of the team and raise her status in the company. I gave her all the credit for the turnaround, which she deserved, but my boss knew it was me who made it possible.

Many years later, she tracked me down. She called me from her retirement party and thanked me for giving her that chance. She had enjoyed several more years at that company, feeling proud of the work she was doing and continuing to earn the respect of her peers.

Wow. That phone call was one of the most rewarding moments of my career.

When an underperforming employee hears your concerns and responds, rising to the level of the rest of the team, you have done something profound. You have created real value for your company, and you have saved someone's career. You have helped them overcome whatever obstacle was in their way. You have made them successful and possibly even happy.

Reducing Turnover

It's far better to help an existing employee improve than it is to fire them and bring in someone new.

Remember, someone (you, maybe?) once thought this person worthy of hiring. They joined the team and then something went wrong.

Rather than discard this person, figure out if there is a problem that can be solved.

It may be that there isn't. It may be that defensiveness and insecurity prevent them from making any improvements at all.

But you may discover a systemic problem, or one that you can solve with clear communication of expectations and achievable goals.

Every human being is worth at least one serious attempt at career salvation. (Except for the Outdoer, of course.)

And it's better for you and your team to keep your turnover down.

Lower turnover means you and your team enjoy the benefits of stability. If you've been able to cultivate positive team dynamics, it keeps those in place. No matter how thoroughly you interview, it's always slightly risky to bring in someone new to replace a former employee. Introducing new team members changes the team dynamics, if only for a short while, so low turnover allows you to maintain the culture you've built.

Lower turnover also improves efficiency and productivity. Recruiting takes time—your time—which could better be spent on projects that move the team forward.

And losing a member of the team leaves the group short. For a while, others may be able to pick up extra work to cover for the loss of a teammate, but your group will lose productivity while you are filling the vacancy. And covering for an open position gets old fast. When it goes on too long, it can damage morale and provide people with a legitimate complaint about your management abilities.

Then, once you have brought on your new hire, still more time— yours and theirs—is lost to training. There's the hope that the new person will fit in and positive team dynamics will return quickly. There's also the possibility that they won't fit in and then you have another challenge on your hands.

So overall, reducing turnover and keeping your team together is a good strategy for maintaining productivity and efficiency, and for making your job easier.

As you think about your underperforming employee, get straight in your own head what is going wrong. How is this employee underperforming and exactly what do they need to do to rise to the level of the rest of the team? How can you describe exactly what they are doing wrong and specifically what they need to do to improve? Precisely how you will determine if they are doing it?

This is the beginning of a performance improvement plan, but it's also a good way for you to double-check that the trouble this employee is having is truly of their own making. Are your expectations reasonable? Is there something in the workplace that might affect performance? Is there substance abuse?

Once you're confident that there are no external factors, work with your HR staff to come up with a performance improvement plan—more on those later in Chapter 25.

If things go well, you will have done the right thing by the employee and the company. Your team will see that you didn't rush to judgment, that you supported the employee and gave them every chance to succeed.

And if things don't go well, you need to let them go.

This is one of the reasons you want to be respected but not necessarily liked: as you optimize your team, which is an ongoing process, you will have difficult conversations and you will make difficult decisions. You will be doing the right thing, but you will not win Boss of the Year while you're going through it.

When you're letting someone go, don't expect everyone, even your top performers, to appreciate what you're doing. Though they may have complained about the low achiever, they are not responsible for solving that problem, you are. The team enjoys the luxury of being sympathetic, feeling the pain of losing a co-worker and even thinking you are cold-hearted.

Over time, maybe not even that long, they will come to realize you did the right thing for the right reasons, and you did it in the right way.

Chapter 11: Setting Goals

You've probably been through a performance review. You go to an HR website, then someone—you or your manager—will write down goals and there will be some way of measuring them and some kind of timetable, even if it's just the next performance review.

Maybe you looked at your goals between reviews, maybe not. Maybe your manager looked the other way if you didn't hit one or two of them. And maybe that was the right thing to do. Or maybe neither of you really cared about goals all that much, so it didn't matter.

Sometimes goal setting is seen as obligatory but not particularly helpful. Managers go through the motions, the team plays along, then everyone goes back to work.

But for most teams, the process of discussing, setting and measuring goals can be extremely helpful. The key is putting the goals in the proper context.

Goals are guideposts. They should be treated as reminders of what's important and how your team's work ties in with the rest of the company. They should not feel like an arbitrary, rigid, corporate cram-down.

As long as you treat goals as a framework that guides the team's work, and not as gotchas to trap and punish employees, as some jerk managers might do, goals are very productive.

In a perfect world, the entire company would be aligned around a mission, strategies, tactics and goals.

The mission of the company is a statement about what differentiates the company in the marketplace. Say, make the safest cars in the world (as opposed to the fastest, best-looking, cheapest, etc.).

Strategies are the general, long-term ways the company is going to execute the mission statement, particularly as regards the competition. One strategy for our imaginary car company might be: exceed US passenger safety standards.

Tactics are the specific things employees will do to fulfill the strategies. Develop a side-impact protection system that is twice as effective as required by law, for example.

Your team's goals then outline how your folks will accomplish one or more tactics: install the side-impact hardware for Model Z.

With goals that stem from the company's mission statement, an employee can see that the work they do installing the side-impact system for Model Z directly contributes to the company's differentiator of making the safest cars in the world.

All that would happen in a perfect world. I've never lived in a perfect world. I've never worked for a company that was that well organized or, maybe looked at another way, one that was so rigid in its thinking. But at several of my companies, we did try. And though we fell short of that perfect top-to-bottom alignment, the result was still a very good framework that helped each employee understand how their work was contributing to the overall success of the company.

Start by drafting up a list of goals. Talk with your people about how they relate to the company's tactics and strategies. Ask for your team's input and listen to what they have to say. You may learn that some of the goals you've set are not achievable, or that your timetable is off. You may hear suggestions for measuring progress or even setting the bar higher than you did.

By inviting the group to get involved with goal setting, you are giving them a stake in the process. It's tough for someone to complain later that the goals were unrealistic when they were involved in setting them.

As you decide on each goal, talk about how you will measure progress, and what timeline is reasonable for each.

Measurability is key. Be sure to construct your goals so that they can be measured objectively. The entire process of setting goals can be turned upside down if, in the end, there is disagreement about whether or not a goal was met.

This is particularly true when goals are used to determine compensation, as in many sales organizations. Good salespeople are creative, and they will try to apply that creativity to the interpretation of their goals. Their goals must be very clear and measurable and unarguable. The more complicated your commission structure, the more loopholes you will probably create, so think carefully about unambiguous measurability when laying out your sales compensation plan.

As much as possible, goals should be measured using a number, or "yes," and "no." You either did or did not produce 5,000 devices. You either did or did not increase revenue by 5%. You either did or did not improve your customer satisfaction score.

For much of my career, I managed creative teams, and it's really not possible to define and measure creativity. Creativity is completely subjective, as is any product stemming from a creative process—in the eye of the beholder, and all that.

But we could measure volume—the amount of creative product we produced. We could also measure whether people met deadlines. We could measure development of specific skills. Each of these things related directly to the success of the team and the company, and we avoided arguing over whether or not work was creative enough.

In addition to these kinds of non-creative tasks, there was the big question: did the company succeed or not during the period? Obviously, the company's success, or the lack of it, was only partly the result of my team's efforts, but I thought it was still important to measure and discuss it as a reminder of how important our work was. It's easy to get into the weeds and focus exclusively on small things, so lift your head up now and then and remember how important your work is in the big scheme.

In the end, we set and measured goals that worked very well. We weren't directly measuring creativity, but that was OK; we already had an ongoing, nearly daily discussion about creative issues. And the framework our goals provided helped us think about the other things that we could improve, then make a plan to improve them.

Without the goal-setting framework, we might never have taken the time to think seriously about how we worked and what changes we could make to become better.

Our goals helped to create a culture of continuous improvement: observation, analysis and action.

When you work with your team to set goals, as with any collaborative process, don't expect consensus. You can't please everyone. Not everyone will agree with every goal. After listening, you will need to make the call. And when you do, explain your reasoning.

When everyone feels they've been heard and when you've taken their points into consideration, they will generally understand when you arrive at a reasonable and fair decision even if it's not what they had in mind.

Goal setting can work for any kind of any team. Even if they're involved in routine work over which they have little control, you can set goals for safety, workplace cleanliness, or other things that will improve their work experience. In this case, the input from your team is likely to be very relevant. They know best what they'd like to improve and probably have some good ideas about how to go about it.

I've seen things like employee suggestion boxes, town hall meetings, safety committees and newsletters come from teams that otherwise had routine tasks.

Also, read your team. Some people just like to do a good job. They don't necessarily want to be a part of a goals discussion or talk about measurability. As long as they know their input is welcome, let them be. If they complain about the goals later, gently remind them they might consider being a part of the process next time.

When you have defined your goals and the way they will be measured and the timeline for evaluation, write it all up using clear, unambiguous language. There should be no room for misinterpretation.

Then let your team take another look. Make sure everyone is clear on the meaning of each goal and what they need to do to help the team achieve it.

If you think of goals as a framework rather than an obligation, you may find yourself looking at the goals and the team's progress several times during the quarter or the year or whatever your timeline dictates. Stay on top of the things you're measuring. If the team is falling behind in any area, make corrections to stay on course.

It's OK to change your goals mid stream. If the business climate changes or the company launches new initiatives or products, double-check to see that your goals still fit. If not, get together with your boss and your team and figure out what changes to make.

Once your goals are set and your team is working towards hitting them, look for milestones to celebrate. If you need to make 5,000 widgets, and halfway through the year you've already made 3,000, take a moment to congratulate everyone for being on track to exceed the goal.

When the year is up, get together again and discuss each goal. Did you meet them or exceed them? If so, talk about why. If some fortunate but unexpected thing helped you overachieve, see if you can build it into your plan for the next cycle.

Did you fall short? Talk about that too. Figure out what prevented your team from hitting the goal and what you can do to solve that problem the next time.

If performance problems contributed to missing a goal, address them right away but do it privately. Praise publicly, critique privately.

There may be external problems. It's OK to say sales only increased by 3%, not 5%, because there was a problem with production that prevented your sales team from fulfilling all their orders. The goal was not met, but it was because of circumstances beyond their control.

At least your team knows they did well, and they will be motivated to do it again next quarter or next year. And your company now knows where they need to concentrate their efforts. The production group needs attention, not the sales team.

No need to vilify the production folks. In fact, be supportive of their efforts. Just make sure your team knows their work is appreciated even though the company missed the goal.

Unfortunately, if a bonus was tied to hitting that 5% increase, it may not matter that your team did their part. The bonus fund may have depended on the full increase in sales, so the money may not be there, regardless of the reason.

Hopefully, your company is enlightened enough not to punish your top performers for sub-par results that were out of their control. If the full bonus isn't possible but your team did their part, do something to reward their hard work, even if it's just taking them out to lunch. The acknowledgment is important, though not as important as cash, of course. But doing something is better than doing nothing at all.

The bottom line is this: don't think of goals as a tedious corporate obligation. Don't just check that box and move on. The goals process is filled with communication, listening, respect, and collaboration. Just the things that will help to build morale and cement your image as a good manager.

Things Nobody Will Tell You
Insubordination

Insubordination is a charge that has been used improperly against employees for so long I believe it's no longer valid.

Insubordination is the refusal to carry out a reasonable task assigned by your manager. But instead, it's often used to punish employees for what my great aunt used to call "back talk."

You want to have open and honest communication with your team with as few barriers as possible. Introducing the possibility of insubordination—something a manager might whip out anytime a conversation takes an uncomfortable turn—puts up a pretty big barrier.

Is it insubordinate to disagree with a manager? It shouldn't be. Managers should welcome other viewpoints and be strong enough not to take it personally when someone voices one. That's how you learn and course correct. Smart teams speak up when they feel valued and respected and want to do the right thing for the business.

Is it insubordinate to tell a manager you believe they are making a mistake? Hopefully not. Managers are human and mistakes happen. You want your team to have your back, just like you have theirs, and to prevent you from taking a wrong turn.

When an employee comes to you with a concern, it means several good things: you have done a good job of earning their trust; you have created a culture of open communication; your team cares about your success and wants to help you avoid a misstep; and you have empowered your team to think beyond their job descriptions.

Of course, you can undo all that goodness by reacting like an insecure boob, taking the input as a personal affront, getting defensive and tossing out accusations of insubordination. That's exactly what a jerk manager would do.

Good luck trying to earn back the trust you just lost.

Don't confuse insubordination with disruption or negligence. If a team member is acting in a disruptive manner or if they fail to perform without justification, address it firmly. Just call these problems what they are rather than using the vague, archaic charge of insubordination.

Chapter 12: Your Team's Brand

> Over half of respondents (53.6 percent) state the top reason that keeps them from quitting their job is the loyalty they feel to their team, boss, coworkers or their company.
>
> *recruiting firm Accounting Principals*

When talking about my team, particularly to my boss and my peers, I like to think in marketing terms. I want my team to have a brand. I want people to have an image in their heads whenever they think about my team or its members.

You react to brands all the time. All you have to do is to hear a company name and you'll automatically have a brand image in your head:

> Porsche = high performance
> Whole Foods = healthy eating
> Rolex = quality and status

I want my group to be thought of as, "High-Competence-Low-Drama," and I look for every opportunity to send and reinforce that message with my boss and my management peers. Of course, before I can run around making that claim, I need my people to live up to it.

That's one of the first conversations I'll have with a new team and with a new team member. I don't necessarily use the term "brand," but I let them know I want people to think of this team as highly competent and professional. I tell them that this is for them, not me. It's about making them look good. I tell them I intend to promote them to my boss and to everyone else in the company, but I need them on board because I need it to be true.

Most people have never heard a manager talk that way. Most have never thought of a team as having an identity. Many have never heard of a boss promoting them to others in the company. And most get on board right away. After all, who wouldn't want to be thought of as a highly skilled non-whiner?

This is very different from a manager who "sets a high bar" and "demands excellence." All that bar-setting and demanding is being done by the manager, and it's obvious who's going to get the credit when the team puts in the extra effort.

The brand conversation also sets high performance goals, but it's for the benefit of each of my folks, not me. They need to perform so they will be associated with a positive brand and I can promote their efforts and increase their stature in the company.

This is usually spectacularly successful. People quickly develop pride in their group and the product they turn out. As everyone comes together around the brand, I start mentioning individuals to my boss and noting team-wide accomplishments. Gradually this builds that brand image in the boss's mind.

Once my team sees evidence of my efforts to promote them, which thanks to Law of Management #3, *Everyone Knows Everything*, happens almost immediately, their determination to make the brand true increases even more.

And the impact it has on others in the company is profound as well. Unsolicited, I've had bosses ask if there's something special they can do for my team since they're performing so well. I've had people from other parts of the company quietly approach me to see if there might be an opportunity with my group. My people have been stopped in the hallway by other managers and congratulated for something I mentioned earlier in a management meeting.

And of course, my own reputation benefitted significantly. I have never attempted to claim credit for my team's hard work. I give all the credit to them, individually and as a group. But people know. My boss knows my employees don't complain to HR, we hit our goals, we're not whiners. To be honest, this approach has served me very well.

The amazing thing is that it all ends up being true. What starts as a marketing concept, a brand, ends up becoming a reality as the team lives up to the brand.

(I'm astonished when I hear managers complain about their teams or make fun of people who report to them. Maybe they think that somehow makes them look good, though I don't know how it can since they're in charge of the people they're whining about. And what kind of brand is that creating?)

Naturally, as with all brands, there are occasional off-brand moments. It's important to let your people know when they are not living up to the image you are trying to project. In my case, it's often the "Low-Drama" part of the brand that gets people into trouble. But a quick conversation usually turns things around.

Another good thing about having a brand is you eventually build brand equity. That's a reserve of goodwill that gets you through rough patches. With brand equity, people will simply assume your team is performing well all the time. If you stumble a bit, they may not even notice, or if they do, they'll think it's an aberration.

Your entire team benefits from a strong team brand, including your low performers, which is another reason to make sure everyone on the team deserves to be there. It's hard to be proud of your group when you have folks who simply aren't at the same level as the rest. So that means you need to work with your low performers to bring them up or you need to move them out.

More to come on that topic later in the book.

Section 3: Running Your Team

You've come a long way already! In just a few pages, you've developed a new way of looking at your role as a manager:

- You know the Laws of Management
- You understand what a jerk manager is and why you don't want to be one
- You are working to keep your ego in check and your focus on the team
- You have evaluated your own personality and resolved to do any internal work necessary
- You have thoroughly evaluated your team and your boss, and you have a good understanding of the people you're working with and how to deal with them

Now let's talk about the things you'll do day in and day out as you manage your team, your boss and your peers.

Chapter 13: Communication

Your communication skills will have a direct impact on your career success. Clear communication is a critically important part of being a manager. It enables you to earn respect, it helps employees to do their jobs better and feel good about the company. It keeps the team on track, and it helps your boss appreciate what you do.

Done right, communication makes your team run smoother, your job easier and your boss happier.

Done poorly, which usually means not done enough, it can leave your team feeling isolated, degrade their performance and cast doubt on your management abilities.

But good communication doesn't just happen. It's the result of planning, understanding how you will be heard, and choosing the right medium.

Communication with your team helps them to have confidence in your leadership. It gives you the opportunity to show that you support them. It helps build mutual respect.

Communication with your boss does the same things—builds confidence in your abilities, shows you support them and builds trust and respect.

But communication is a very human endeavor, and because it's human, it's prone to misunderstandings and misinterpretations and can easily fail entirely. As a manager, you need to understand how and how much to communicate with each member of your team and with your boss. You need to understand what information will be valuable and what will be distracting. You want to be sure your message is getting through and is interpreted the way you intend.

In short, you want to deliver value when you communicate, so people will look forward to hearing from you and they will open your next email or happily agree to your next meeting.

Communicating with the Boss

As a general rule, it's best to communicate with the boss more rather than less. Frequent, brief updates give your boss confidence that you're managing your team well and that you don't need babysitting. The more your boss hears about your team's successes, the more appreciation they will have for the talents of your people and the skillful way you are managing them.

Depending on your boss, you may get feedback or confirmation that they've received and read the updates. You also may not, but a lack of confirmation doesn't mean the boss isn't reading them.

However, if you discover your boss isn't paying attention to the updates you send, you can adjust their length and frequency or follow up verbally. Part of communicating is making sure you're being heard, so fine-tune your plan and keep the information flowing in a way that works for your manager.

Make no mistake, this is all on your shoulders. If your boss is surprised by something, and you've tried but failed to make them aware of it, it's still your fault. Saying, "But I sent you an email, didn't you read it?" is not a good boss management strategy.

Here are a couple of things to consider putting in those periodic updates to the corner office:

Reinforcement of and progress toward the team's goals. This should not be a rehash of previous discussions about strategy or goals but rather a gentle reminder of the path you're on and how the team is progressing toward those goals. The reason to do this is both to let your boss know the team is doing well and to give them an opportunity to tell you if things are changing so you can adjust if necessary.

If something's getting in your team's way and the deliverables or schedules are in jeopardy, let your boss know as early as possible. They may be able to help remove obstacles and can reset expectations with other parts of the company.

Promotion of the team. Make sure your boss knows when someone on your team does something particularly well. This not-so-subtly reinforces that you are a good manager, and it may result in your boss recognizing the team member, which can be great for morale.

Also, be sure to let the boss know when good things happen to your team, like winning an award or taking on a community service project. These are the kinds of things good managers like to pass on to their bosses.

Don't be boastful about this, just make sure it's clear which team member deserves a pat on the back.

Over time, you'll get a sense of how much communication is too much for your boss and you can adjust accordingly.

I've had bosses who like weekly updates, and others who respond better to quick one- or two-sentence notes when there's something worth sharing.

I've never had a boss who liked (or read) dense, long updates.

Periodic updates are not the place to put urgent or important information. Your manager may not read regular updates immediately or may only skim them. If there is something important you want your boss to know right away, it requires its own email, phone call, or in-person conversation.

Communicating with Your Team

A team that hears from their manager frequently feels in touch, supported and valued. And there's a lot more to talk about than you may realize.

Let your team know how they're doing. Are they hitting the milestones outlined in their goals? Are there any big wins to celebrate? Can you pass on a compliment from someone in the company? When you give your group updates on their performance, it helps them to appreciate the importance of their roles and shows them you're on top of the details.

Update your team on what's happening in the company (without disclosing confidential information, of course). Let them know about executives joining or leaving the company, about new products or marketing campaigns. Hearing company news from you is far better than reading about it in a trade publication.

Give your people a heads-up when visitors will come by, or when investors are taking a tour. Strangers prowling around the workplace can make people nervous, so your team will appreciate knowing what's going on in advance.

Each time you walk out of your management meeting, ask yourself whether you learned anything that your folks should know about. The more they know about the issues you face, the more context they'll have and the better they'll understand management's decisions.

Be sure to share the successes of other teams or departments so your folks can appreciate the good work being done in other areas of the company.

Keep up with news about your industry and bring those updates to your team. Well-informed employees can help come up with ideas that propel the business forward. Particularly when times get tough, people want to help, not just become victims of circumstance. Good knowledge of industry trends helps everyone understand the challenges facing the business and enables them to think about solutions.

If practical, have regular staff meetings with your people. These don't have to be big, orchestrated affairs. Getting together gives you a chance to provide updates in person. Be sure to allow time on the agenda for an open forum so people can ask questions or raise issues.

Have individual conversations with your employees frequently. Talk about how things are going for them and let them know if there is something they can do to improve. These informal discussions give employees a chance to improve their performance without waiting for a formal review. No one should be surprised by something they hear in a review—they should already know how you view their strengths and what they need to work on.

Ask each of your people for their views on the team, the company and you. Employees rarely volunteer their thoughts about these things, but when you ask, it's often surprising what you hear.

If you're dealing with problem employees, talk to HR about documenting these informal conversations. That way if an employee claims to be shocked about something in a review, or says a performance improvement plan comes out of nowhere, you'll be able to show that you've been keeping them updated all along.

More communication is always better than less, so keep it coming. Your group will appreciate it and it will help build trust in your honest, open leadership.

When There's Big News

When you're working hard on big projects or making big changes to your organization, it's surprisingly easy to get caught up in that important work and forget about the other part of your job—taking care of the people who report to you. While you're off doing whatever it is you need to do, your team is aware that something's going on. If you aren't talking to them, they'll wonder why they're being kept in the dark.

When people think something's happening but they don't know what it is, they assume it's going to be bad. They're usually right, by the way. Layoffs, mergers, reorganizations—all those things are schemed up in secret. Then one day there's a mysterious company meeting or an announcement to the press and only then do employees find out their fate.

Meanwhile, everyone knows something's coming but nobody knows what it is, and they're not happy. How much productivity will be lost, how badly will morale be damaged and how long will it take to restore trust? If you have an adversary on your team, they'll be vindicated: all the secrecy and suspicion will reinforce their belief that the company is out to screw its employees.

So unless you're working on something that really must be done in complete secrecy, it's very important to keep your team in the loop as much as you can.

Sometimes it's not a need for secrecy but simple negligence that leaves employees feeling out of the loop.

I once knew a manager who got so wrapped up in his own reorganization planning that he forgot to let his team know about essential things like schedule changes and reassignments. Even the people whose schedules were changing or who were being reassigned had no idea until he remembered to tell them a few hours before the changes took effect.

Then they had to scramble and scrap their personal plans to accommodate the new schedule they should have known about weeks earlier.

That's an excellent way to alienate your team, and it's completely unnecessary. Just take a few minutes to think about how the things you're working on will affect your team, then let them know as soon as you can.

When There's Bad News

Communicating is a little trickier when the news you have to share is bad. This is particularly true if your industry is mature or declining. To use a realistic example, when there are layoffs at a competitor, your

101

team may understandably become nervous that the same thing could happen to them. It's your job to talk them through the news and give them the company's perspective. Don't do this on your own, though.

First, talk to your boss. Topics like layoffs (or mergers or acquisitions or bankruptcies) should be handled carefully. You don't want to spook your people, but you don't want them to be caught off guard either, and you definitely don't want to be out of sync with the management team.

Work with your boss to come up with a way to provide the company's perspective. How is your company different from the one that had the layoffs? Whether or not layoffs are possible in your organization, talk to your boss about how to answer that question when it comes up, because it will. You don't want to say there will never be layoffs—who knows that for sure?—but you don't want to scare people either. The best way is to be tactfully honest, but coordinate important communication like that with your manager.

There are many factors that influence what you are able to say. You don't want to be the one who opens their mouth and messes up an acquisition negotiation. Public companies have to be careful about information that might affect the markets or influence investors. That's why it's important to stay in sync with your boss and peers when handling potentially sensitive information.

Once you know what you're going to say, you have a couple options for saying it. If it's not urgent, relay the information in a way that is natural and logical, like in a routine staff meeting. This allows you to say what you have to say without raising an alarm, which is what happens when you suddenly call a special meeting.

If you need to call a special meeting, announce and hold it quickly. Don't give people time to worry and speculate about what might be coming.

Of course, before communicating sensitive information to your folks, apply Law of Management #3: *Everyone Knows Everything*. As soon as your team knows what's going on, so will everyone else in the company. And that goes both ways. If another manager is talking to their team, that conversation will get back to your people fast. And by "fast," I mean the time it takes to send a text.

Communication Cautions

Constant, thorough communication is essential to managing a team, but you must still use caution.

First, never write anything that you wouldn't want to be made public. Anything you write or email or text or message can end up in places you don't anticipate, so never write anything that would embarrass you or your company if it became public.

This seems obvious, but clearly it's not. Many very smart executives and savvy politicians have sent emails and texts that have caused enormous damage to their organizations and careers, so think hard before hitting "Send" and always, always take the high road.

Second, never communicate personal information or opinions, no matter what the format. Don't make fun of your team members, your boss, or yourself. Don't be political. Don't tell jokes. Keep all communication professional at all times. It can be tempting to go for a laugh or to try to bond with your team over an intra-company rivalry, or to poke gentle fun at other managers.

Don't do it.

Anything you say or write will get out eventually. Even if it doesn't (but really, it will) there's no way taking the high road can cause you trouble.

Things that seem benign when you write them can have a way of looking really bad out of context, so just keep it professional.

I once left a voice mail for one of my peers expressing–in what I'll call a passionate way–my disappointment at the way something had turned out. Well, the charming guy played that message for our boss the next morning. I had no problem with the boss knowing I was disappointed, but with him, I certainly would have chosen different words to express that disappointment. That was not my finest moment.

This is hard because we're not accustomed to censoring our texts or emails. The impulse to go for a quick laugh or to be a little too honest is a strong one. We like it when our personality comes out in our messages. But you really must curb those urges for your own good. Keep your messages informative but boring.

And it may be best not to send a message at all. There are times when a phone call may be far preferable. The reason is simple: everything else leaves a trail.

Texts, emails, messages and written notes never really die. There's a reason emails from corporate attorneys often go like this:

"Call me."

I've found that more than anyone else in the company, attorneys know that documenting conversations in email can complicate things.

Sometimes it's best to think like an attorney and pick up the phone.

Don't Overfill Your Five-Pound Bag

Whether you're talking with someone or writing an email, assume people can retain, at most, three main points, so limit your communication to just three concepts. And there are times when even that can be too many. Sometimes just a single message is best, particularly for important, difficult or radical concepts.

"We should consider outsourcing our manufacturing," is a huge concept, and will trigger several related conversations, so don't attempt to cover anything more than that.

For more routine communication, think of the "3 by 3" rule: three concepts with up to three supporting facts for each.

Here's how a routine update for the boss might look following this rule:

1. The team won an award from the National Association of Corporate Recognition on Friday
    - The award was for Outstanding Award Submission, and we beat teams from several of our competitors
    - Micaela and Alex were singled out for their contributions
    - We will receive a plaque that we can add to our awards case in the lobby
2. My team continues their safe workplace streak, having just crossed the 500-incident-free-days milestone
    - The company's workplace safety training has increased my team's awareness of safety issues
    - We're celebrating this milestone with ice cream at our next staff meeting

3. I'm encouraging people to take vacations over the next couple of months
   - The workload is relatively light right now, but that will change by October
   - Several folks have a lot of vacation time banked, so this will give them a chance to draw that down
   - By having everyone start their planning now, I'll be able to schedule so that they can take the time they want and we will still be covered over the summer

Remember to leave lots of space between lines and avoid off-putting blocks of dense text.

Things Nobody Will Tell You
Don't Be a Downer

There is a cumulative effect of communication that you need to manage. If you find that you are often bringing your boss (or your client) bad news and you aren't able to balance that with lots of good news, you will become branded as a downer. Once that happens, people will start to suspect that you're an overly pessimistic person. They may try to avoid interactions with you since they're often too negative. They will wonder if you're the cause of this bad news instead of just the bearer of it, that perhaps someone else in your role would do a better job of avoiding all the bad things that are happening.

So be sure you have good news far more often than bad. Keep the ratio at 10 to 1 or better.

One useful tactic is to arrange for the bad news to come from someone else. A manager who's less savvy than you are might be willing to bring the bad news to the boss and allow you to keep your ratio going.

I once had a great boss who said, "Good news, us...bad news, them." Words to live by.

This is less of a concern when dealing with your team, where you still need to think about balancing the good with the bad but your focus on open and honest communication needs to come first.

Chapter 14: Making Meetings Meaningful

Meetings can be interesting and informative, or they can be horrible and tedious. Your people can leave them feeling smarter, or they can leave them wishing they'd called in sick. It's completely up to you.

Some managers think of meetings as opportunities to perform. Insert obligatory laughter here.

Some managers don't like them but are told to have them, so they say a few words and end them as quickly as possible.

I've had managers who encouraged debate and loved hearing differing opinions. I've had others who look at you when you speak up as though you'd just spit in their soup.

The point of meetings is not just to assemble—and certainly not to watch the boss perform—but to provide information to the team, have them provide information to you and to each other, and to discuss issues that are important to multiple team members. Meetings ensure everyone hears the same thing at the same time and give everyone a chance to participate in important discussions.

Meetings also give you an opportunity to observe. You'll be able to recognize body language and know when people are uncomfortable with what's being said even if they don't speak up, giving you a reason to follow up one-on-one at another time.

As with any other interaction you have with your team, meetings should be all about them. Give them information you think they will find useful. Have them update you and each other. Debate issues that affect them all or release those who aren't involved and continue on with those who are.

Respect your team's time. Take a few minutes prior to the meeting to prepare an agenda, then use it to guide the meeting. Allow for a little relevant deviation from the agenda but be wary of conversations that get off-topic or involve only a few participants. When the discussion veers off course gently guide it back but let everyone know you will revisit the topic you cut short at another time. In other words, don't appear to dismiss someone's concerns for the sake of the agenda.

As always, keep your ego in check, don't take things personally, don't get defensive. Let people express themselves and don't publicly criticize them. If you hear a comment or see behavior that needs to be addressed, make a note and follow up later.

Meetings are great opportunities for show and tell. From time to time, assign a team member to prepare a presentation about what they're working on. Think about visual things you can share. Do you have samples of the company's new marketing campaign? Are there product designs you can show? Interesting growth charts or investor presentations or sales figures everyone might want to see?

Keep things interesting by having theme meetings. Once in a while, drop the regular agenda and do something special. It's kind of like showing up for English class and discovering there's a movie for the entire period.

Depending on your group's role, it might make sense to bring in guests. People from other parts of the company, outside advisors or visiting executives can make good guests. Just make sure they are prepared to say something interesting and then come armed with several questions you can use to jump-start a Q&A session.

Keep your meetings moving, and when you're done, end them. There's nothing more painful for your people than meetings that drag on too long. Follow your agenda, make sure people who have something to say are heard, and wrap things up. There's no shame in a short but productive meeting.

Just because you scheduled the meeting for an hour doesn't mean it has to run that long. End it when it's over, even if that's 20 minutes in.

On the other hand, don't let your meeting run long. If you are at the scheduled end time and there's more to cover, schedule another meeting involving the people who need to be there. Busy people will plan other things following your meeting, so don't throw their schedules into chaos by running long.

Also, ask yourself why you could not accomplish your agenda in the time you scheduled. Did the meeting go off course? Did you pack too much into your agenda? Did you uncover new information that needed discussion?

See if there's something you can learn and if so, don't make the same mistake again.

Scheduling Meetings

When you pick a time for your meetings, think about your team's routines. Don't call people in early or ask them to stay late just to attend your meeting unless you're paying them extra for their time and giving them plenty of notice.

If your team covers multiple shifts, change your schedule to meet on their timetable, even if it means one meeting per shift and a couple of long days for you. You're letting people know that you care about their time and respect their lives outside of work.

If you have team members spread out across time zones, vary the meeting time so the same people aren't inconvenienced over and over.

Some managers think it's fun to hold meetings in outdoor spaces. If you work for a company with nice grounds or one that has a park nearby, you may be tempted to take your meeting outside. Unless there's a reason to be outside—like, you're meeting about the landscaping or the building is on fire—don't do it. It's noisy and there is one distraction after another. You'll either end your meeting early because nobody can hear or it'll drag on forever as you try to recapture peoples' attention over and over.

Remember, a meeting is a forum for useful, strategic communication. Keep it professional and don't waste anyone's time.

Management Team Meetings

If your boss is like most, they will hold regular meetings with you and your management peers.

The boss will handle these meetings however they want to, and therefore what you do in those meetings will be up to them. Do you speak up? Raise issues? Keep your mouth shut? Laugh on cue? It's up to the boss.

No matter what, the usual rules apply: don't get defensive, don't take things personally, promote your team and don't be a jerk.

If the boss encourages discussion and if decisions will be made in these meetings, you have some homework to do.

This may sound more like advice for politicians than for managers, but think of the management team meeting as a place to formalize discussions you've already had. Never raise an issue in a meeting unless you know how the conversation will turn out.

Let's say your team has an idea for a new product, and you want the management team to agree to develop a prototype and conduct a consumer trial. You know doing this right will mean lots of people have to sign on: product design, research, marketing, finance and production or engineering or whoever will have to make the prototype.

Long before the management meeting, meet with your peers one-on-one. Present your idea to them, show the potential benefits, get them thinking about their role in pulling off the trial. Take your time, work with them to get their support. Once you have some input and a sense of the cost, include the boss—take their temperature and if they seem receptive, keep going.

Figure out who's with you and who's not and make a judgment call about whether you have the support you need to get your idea off the ground. If you decide to go forward, let the boss and everyone who's in favor know that you plan to bring this project up in the next management meeting.

Don't warn the nay-sayers.

Then go for it. If you've done your prep work and you have people on your side going into the meeting, the conversation will go your way. The boss may give you a green light on the spot, or you may get sent to do some more work, but both are wins.

Your idea didn't get killed, and those who oppose it saw how much support you have. You stacked the deck in your favor, and you used the meeting to turn the plan into action.

Though the boss may say they want their meetings to be forums for debate, you don't. You want the debate to be over by the time the meeting starts. The last thing you want to do is pop out with an important idea in a management meeting not knowing who your friends are.

Chapter 15: Managing Your Boss

Oh, how I wish I had known more about boss management when I started my management career. I wish I could have seen myself through my boss's eyes back then, put myself in the boss's shoes and seen myself as an employee. Would I want to manage someone like me? If not, what should I be doing differently to make me easier to manage?

Managing up is essential, but it can be time-consuming and difficult. If you're lucky enough to have a good manager, managing up might be pretty simple. If you have a manager who is insecure, credit-hungry, a poor communicator or some combination of all of these, this is not going to be easy.

Managing up helps ensure your boss will support you and your team. It gives your boss the information they need to be successful with their bosses.

As we discussed in Chapter 6, some bosses like to keep their involvement at a very high level. Others want to know all the details. Some bosses want to avoid conflict. Others believe conflict is constructive, even if it's also painful.

Many bosses will love that you're able to put your ego aside and manage your team in a way that makes them happy and productive. They'll appreciate that you put the company first, have low turnover and high employee engagement. They may see that your team's feedback on management surveys is unusually positive.

Some bosses will believe you should crack the whip. They'll think treating employees like human beings is coddling them. They'll want you to be a jerk.

Aside from the obvious—you want to avoid working for the whip cracker—you will need to figure out how to manage your boss. And that starts with communication.

Where Do You Stand?

One of the first things you need to do is figure out where you are. If you're in a new company, does your boss have any biases or preconceptions about you based on others who have been in your role? What are the boss's expectations? Are people in your job supposed to be creative or clever or aggressive? Think about whether you want to reinforce that perception or gradually change it.

If you and your boss have been together for a while, you should have a good idea of what your boss thinks of you. Those perceptions can be very difficult to change, and you may not need to, but at least think about where you are. If you do want to make a change, you will need to signal that to the boss.

Perceptions don't change on their own, so in addition to improving your team, you need to let the boss know *you're* improving. It can be as simple as saying, "I've been thinking that there might be a better way of doing things," or "A friend of mine in a related industry is doing things a little differently and I think maybe we can benefit from those changes too." Signaling the change makes the boss aware that they may need to reevaluate the way they see you and sets expectations that more communication is coming.

In one of my roles, my group was considered the creative group. While that sounds good, in some respects it ended up being a negative. We were seen as the fun people, but we weren't always considered essential to the product or to the sales effort. My team had some great creative thinkers who had some big ideas about the company and the industry, but it was hard to be taken seriously because we were just the creative people. Big thoughts came from product or sales.

So, I worked with my peers in product and sales to integrate some of my team's ideas. In both cases, I was working with confident leaders who had open minds, and when these new ideas worked, everyone looked good. My team got even more involved and eventually, we were given responsibility for parts of the product and for some of the sales effort. We were playing a non-traditional role, but that was necessary in order to raise our stature in the company and make us essential to the business in the eyes of my boss.

When the boss realized how we were all working together, he quickly saw the political benefit of being in charge of teams that innovate both the product and their own roles, and we were no longer dismissed as the fun but non-essential creative group.

So be aware of where you stand and if you decide that's not good enough, make a plan to evolve.

Set Goals

I know, here we go with goals again, but working with your boss to set your team's goals will clarify their expectations, and reveal the things they need to be successful with their bosses. It also gives you a framework for future communication when you review your team's progress throughout the year.

Not all bosses are good about communicating with their people when things change, so the goals conversation may prompt the boss to mention changes in the business that affect the goals and the work of your team. The sooner you know about that, the better.

Promote Your Team

Remember the team brand you're trying to develop. Look for opportunities to reinforce your brand images—professionalism, innovation, creativity, whatever they may be. Obviously, this is best done subtly, with you providing consistent information over time and the boss forming their impressions. You can't write the team brand in an email and send it to your boss. You need to earn it bit by bit, so be consistent.

This is important: never say anything bad about someone on your team unless you are prepared to get rid of them.

Once your boss hears from you that there's a problem with someone on your team, the clock starts ticking. They will expect you to fix it right away—provide training, get rid of the low performer, do something to solve the problem that you just highlighted. If you don't act fast, your boss will start to think you are a weak manager.

That said, if you have a low performer and are going to work with HR to improve their performance, it's better for your boss to hear about that from you than from HR. This is not the same as complaining about someone on your team, it's letting the boss know you're a good manager who has identified a team member who's not up to par and you're taking steps to fix that problem.

Help the Boss Look Good

Just like you, your boss has a boss, and they want to be sure they are making a good impression. Do your best to find out what your boss needs to show how well their teams are performing, then come up with those things as often as possible.

Early in my career, I started a new job with a manager who was in his first big leadership role. I had a marketing background, while he came from another part of the industry. Once, in a casual conversation about our marketing plan, I made a point that was obvious to me but that he'd never thought of before.

Remember, a good manager is willing to learn from their team, and he took this conversation to heart.

Soon after, I heard his boss making that same point during a presentation. My boss had used the information I gave him to make an impression on his boss, who in turn used it to make an impression on his audience. I had influenced the organization, and because my point was recognized by upper management, I got support that made my job a little bit easier.

It didn't matter that I wasn't getting credit for my insight—my boss knew where it came from—but hearing my words come out of someone else's mouth told me I'd done a good job identifying and communicating the right piece of information.

More importantly, I now knew the kind of thing my boss found valuable and saw it pay off for him. I was able to do this several more times, and each time I did I got a little more support for my team because the company increasingly understood our needs.

Another example: I once had a boss who sent a weekly report to her manager listing all her team's success stories for that week. It might have been a little unexpected cost savings, a small competitive triumph or an employee who did something exceptional in the community. She wanted her boss to know how well her business unit was running (and by extension what a good manager she was and what a good team she had) so she delivered a constant drumbeat of good news—achievement, competence, innovation, success, over and over.

Naturally, I made sure my team made her list as often as possible.

Here are the three things I wish somebody had told me when I got my first management job: try to see yourself as your boss sees you; promote your team; help your boss to look good with theirs.

Chapter 16: Managing Managers

There are two categories of managers you'll deal with in your career. The first group consists of managers who report to you. The second comprises your management team peers. As you might expect, the way you handle them couldn't be more different.

Employee-Managers

Just like individual contributors, your employee-managers need your support and trust, and you need to earn theirs. But they differ from individual contributors in an important way: they manage a team of their own, and so they have a greater influence over the culture of your group than any individual member.

Manage your employee-manager the same way you want your boss to manage you. Be honest and supportive, set clear, measurable goals, expect them to live up to your team brand. Stay engaged, but don't micromanager or meddle. Make sure their team is hitting their milestones and keep your ear to the ground, just in case.

As you coach and mentor your employee-managers, also get to know their teams. The last thing you want to do is isolate them from the rest of your group. You don't want them to feel like they are second-class in any way. If you've developed a strong team brand, they'll want to feel like they are a part of that brand too. You want the pride associated with your team to rub off on these folks, so don't let there be a barrier between you and this team.

However, don't undermine your employee in the process. Their team should get to know and trust you and to feel like they can come to you if they need to, but don't accomplish this at the expense of your manager's leadership.

This is a serious balancing act.

You don't want your employee-manager to feel you're cutting them out, but you need to be available for members of their team. You want to support your employee, but you also want to help them course-correct if things start going awry.

One way to help your employee-manager be comfortable with all this open communication is to tell them whenever someone on their team has come to you. They'll find out anyway, so let them know that you've spoken to one of their people and what the topic was. The vast majority of the time, conversations with these teams will be casual, like small talk or broad business issues, so letting your manager know about these conversations helps them to realize they're harmless. They'll come to realize there's no need to panic when their folks talk to you.

Then when you're talking with people who report to your employee, it's important that you listen, but not act. Don't reverse a decision your employee has made, don't express doubt about your employee's judgment or abilities, don't let anyone feel they can bypass their boss and deal directly with you. Be supportive of your employee, and if you hear anything that causes concern, address it later in private in a way that doesn't send them off to punish their talkative team member. Depending on the seriousness of the issue, consider keeping the source's identity confidential.

Also, think about the right amount of integration between your employee's team and your own. Should they all come to your staff meetings? Or should you have one meeting a month that includes everyone? When you send a business update, should that also go to this team? Or should you have your employee-manager pass your updates on while adding some notes of their own?

And be a good boss's boss—congratulate the team or individuals when you hear about exceptional performance, just as you'd like your boss to do with your people.

Your Management Peers

It's useful to think of the management team as a playground of 4th graders.

You'll have brats, bullies, nice kids, nerds, princesses, and wallflowers, and like choosing sides for dodgeball, you have to figure out how to play with each of them. Also like dodgeball, there's a bit of healthy (and sometimes not so healthy) competition between the players.

While the playground metaphor works well for a variety of reasons, it may be more useful to look at the team from your boss's perspective. In what categories from Chapter 7 would you and your peers fit?

You'll find that your management team peers run the gamut from trustworthy confidants to venal backstabbers. Many of them will have motives that are perfectly aligned with the company's success, but a few will be career-obsessed and unscrupulous, willing to do whatever it takes to get ahead. And without a doubt, you'll see some world-class ass-kissing.

The trouble is, not everyone is obvious about their intent, so the ladder-climber may seem perfectly friendly until they perceive a threat or see an opportunity.

When joining a new management team, take your time to get to know your peers. Don't rush to judgment and don't be overly trusting. Try to figure out who sees you as competition and who is glad you've arrived, perhaps because it takes some pressure off them. As always, avoid saying anything negative about anyone.

And remember, a little friendly competition between you and your peers is normal and even constructive, just as it is with the people who report to you.

However, at some point in your career, you are going to deal with a management team peer who is just not happy that you're there. For whatever reason, they are going to be difficult to deal with.

This is a good time to remember Law of Management #5: *The Person with the Smallest Ego Wins*. Resist the temptation to engage in all-out warfare with a difficult peer. That rarely ends well for either party. Instead, there are a couple of subtle things you might do to lessen the effect an aggressive manager can have.

First, get to know people on your peers' teams. You will get a great deal of insight into the issues your peers face and how they manage their teams just by having casual conversations with their team members. If you have a reputation as a good manager, you won't have to ask for any information. It will be offered to you freely.

Getting to know the team of an aggressive peer can unnerve them, make them fear that you've discovered their dirty laundry and worry that you might use it against them.

Not that you would do anything like that, but the chance that you might can help keep an insecure, unruly manager in line. And if that manager should instruct their team not to talk to you, you've just won a big battle. The team will see their boss's insecurities on full display.

Second, just like managing an Adversary or a Troublemaker on your own team, your good relationships with others will be a powerful defense. The stronger your relationship with the boss and the rest of the management team, the more an adversarial peer will become isolated and unsuccessful in their attempts to discredit you.

And as the saying goes, never let 'em see you sweat. Give no indication that you're concerned about what this person is doing. Don't attack them or get defensive. Don't give them the satisfaction of knowing that you've even noticed. You're bigger than that, even if they're not.

Things Nobody Will Tell You
Take Credit for Management Projects

The way you handle credit when dealing with your peers should not be the same as when dealing with your team. While talking about your team's successes, always be humble and give your team credit for their accomplishments. But when talking about your contributions to the management team, you must claim an appropriate amount of credit for the work you do because if you don't someone else will.

This doesn't mean grabbing credit unfairly, it just means reinforcing your contributions along with the contributions of others. Let everyone, particularly the boss, know what you've done.

Giving your team all the credit shows you're a good manager. Giving your peers all the credit suggests that you haven't done anything.

Section 4: Hiring and Firing

Hiring is one of the hardest and riskiest things you will do, but it's a skill you need to develop because turnover is unavoidable, no matter how good a manager you are.

Maybe you had a great leader on your team, and you nurtured and promoted them and now they're moving into a management role in your company. Kudos to you. Or maybe the competition hired someone away, or one of your people decided on a career change or to stay at home and be with the family for a while. Maybe you needed to move an underperformer out.

The result: you need to fill an open position with someone who can be at the same level as the rest of your group. This hire needs to be good at their job and a good fit with the values of the team. You want to hire someone you can nurture and grow, who will help the team succeed, who will contribute to the workplace culture and who will be a long-term asset to the company.

And you need to go about finding this person in a way that sets up your new employee for success. Everything that happens during this process should reflect your honesty, integrity and the company's values.

It's a tall order. And it starts with recruiting.

Chapter 17: Recruiting

> "I'd rather interview 50 people and not hire anyone than hire the wrong person."
>
> *Jeff Bezos, founder of Amazon*

Every industry is different, but each one I've worked in has had a network. People know people, they know companies and they know managers. When there's an opening, word gets out. If your company has a good reputation, the network will make recruiting easier. If your company makes a cool product, that will help too. If your company has a good reputation, makes a cool product, and you are recognized as a great manager, it will be easiest of all.

Being a great manager increases the odds that you'll get top applicants. People will want to work for you, and they'll be ready to compete for your openings.

But if you're known as a jerk manager, recruiting will be tougher. You'll get applicants, but they may not be the best available, and they may not be there for the best of reasons.

While good managers will have applicants who really want to work on their teams, jerk managers may get applicants who have trouble getting jobs anywhere else, or who are willing to put up with crappy managers for a couple of years so they can improve their resumes and move on.

Great managers attract top talent. Jerk managers attract "B" players and opportunists.

But let's not get ahead of ourselves. Before you have to worry about the quality of your candidates, you'll need to write a job description and get it out into the wild where your prospective candidates will see it. You'll need to understand your company's compensation structure, benefits package and hiring process. And you need to understand how to work with your Human Resources team.

Using HR

In my experience, HR departments function very differently from company to company. Some of them have robust recruiting systems and are very helpful to managers in screening applicants. Others leave recruiting up to the manager and don't get involved until the offer letter stage.

Some HR departments hold or attend job fairs, collect resumes and meet prospective candidates. They might have campus recruiting efforts. They might have a good process for collecting and evaluating resumes that come in through the company website.

Get to know your HR staff and find out what kind of help they can offer as you go about filling your opening. Know how they work so you can be sure to dovetail your efforts with theirs. They are likely to have processes and paperwork for things like drug tests and background checks. Understand how that all works so you can help your applicant know what to expect, and so you understand the effect on your hiring timeline.

You'll want HR to have a good grasp of the type of candidate you are looking for. Have a conversation with someone in HR about your ideal candidate. Don't just hand them the job description and send them on their way. Let them know the culture your team has or that you're trying to develop. The more subjective information you can add to the objective requirements of the job description, the better HR will be able to help you.

If it's not already a part of their process, consider having HR interview your top candidates. By the time you have a list of finalists, you'll be deep into the weeds with your candidates. HR may bring fresh eyes and see things you've missed.

I once asked an HR executive to interview my top candidate, a guy I really liked who had great references and all the qualifications we needed. I called the HR person after the interview, expecting her to be as effusive as I was about this guy, and heard something very different. She had noticed an edge about him, something that put her off and set her alarm bells ringing. She couldn't say exactly what it was about him, but something didn't feel right.

Because that seemed vague, rather than explore her concerns more fully, I went ahead and made the hire.

Months later, when we were sitting in a mediator's office fighting a charge of unlawful termination, I had to admit she had been right. We won—things had gone badly wrong with this employee and the termination had been completely legit—but it cost us days and days of research, meetings with our attorneys and disruption for my team.

Lesson learned.

In addition to having HR talk to your top candidates, make sure you understand the entire hiring process end to end, right up to the new employee's first day and the onboarding process.

Not that you'll leave everything up to HR. While things like drug screenings and background checks can be handled by HR without involvement from you, when it comes to your employee's experience of the job, particularly their first day, you will want to be very involved. More on that later.

Chapter 18: Make Your Job Descriptions Sell

Your next employee is out there somewhere, and after seeing an ad or hearing about your opening from a friend, your prospective applicant will turn to the job description to see if they think it's right for them. This means the job description is one of the most important things you will create, not only because it outlines the duties and requirements of the job but also because when done right, it tells your future employee a lot about your team and the company.

One thing to remember during the recruiting process: you're always selling. If applicants are excited about the prospect of working on your team, there will be more of them. More choices mean negotiations will be easier. Your new employee will feel fortunate to have scored the job and they will start out on the right foot. Everything your applicant sees should have a bit of sales pitch in it, and that starts with the job description.

Some job descriptions seem like they're written for the existing team, not prospective employees.

"Are you a rock star engineer? Do you code in your sleep? Are you good enough to join our team of superhumans?"

I'd guess that makes the team feel pretty good, but that kind of arrogance can be a turnoff for a prospect with a normal ego.

What about this: "We offer flexible work hours and work-from-home options. Our employee lounge features video games, ping pong and foosball tables."

Sounds lovely, but too much emphasis on perks makes me wonder what the trade-offs are. Does the company think they can offer a lower salary to compensate for all this convenience? Do they expect employees to work nights and weekends for free trail mix?

When you write your job description, put yourself in the position of your ideal applicant. What do they need to know? What else do you want them to know? What other companies are they looking at?

Also, remember that attention spans are short. You need to hook your applicant quickly and draw them into the description.

Start with a headline that broadly describes the job and has a little sales language. Something like, "Join the Finance Team at One of Phoenix's Best Places to Work!"

Then write a brief introduction adding more detail to the job, including the title, and selling the company a bit more: "Western Widgets is looking for an accounts receivables specialist to help our fast-growing company manage our expanding base of customers who love our client-focused service."

"Fast-growing," "expanding," "love," "client-focused." What a great company this must be.

If your HR team has a job description format they want you to follow, there may only be so much you can do, but still attempt to get a little selling in the first few words.

If you have a lot of control over the description, remember to make the first sentence or two sell the company and the position.

Then when you list the job duties—which hopefully you'll do in bullets—be specific but don't be too cute or too dry. Try to convey the personality of your team a bit, but don't go overboard.

It's not possible to provide job description examples that will work for every job or for every company, but the three examples below show the kind of distinction to watch for.

Compare this:
- The project manager helps the team achieve its goals by managing deadlines and dependencies
- The project manager is responsible for timely communication to all stakeholders

To this:
- The project manager keeps our team running smoothly by tracking deadlines and spotting trouble before it happens, and by keeping everyone is in the loop when things change

And this:

- Our project manager is the glue that holds us together and the grease that lets our wheels spin. You are the Dean of Deadlines, the Detector of Dependencies and the Captain of Communication

The first one is dry and includes common but meaningless language: "helps the team achieve its goals." Do you really need to say that? What else would this person do? It's also worded very formally. "Timely communication to all stakeholders," sounds stuffy and generic—and it's unlikely "stuffy and generic" is how you would want to describe your team.

The second one is also straightforward but has casual language like, "spotting trouble," and, "in the loop," that hints at a down-to-earth culture.

The last one may be a little over the top for some companies but might be a perfect fit for a funky creative team.

Which job sounds more interesting to you? Can you picture the kinds of people who work at those companies? Do you have a mental image of the office space? The wording of your job description will communicate much more than the requirements for the position, so make sure it's saying what you want your future employee to hear.

Show the job description to some of your team members and get their input on the tone. They can help you send the right message about the role and the workplace culture.

Also, because job descriptions can be interpreted very literally, your legal team may have some specific language to add, like, "Other duties as assigned," to cover you if things change post-hire. And of course, you will want to follow the company guidelines regarding language about equal employment opportunity and other policies.

Once you've decided on the style of the job description, give careful consideration to the requirements. After reading the job duties, this is the next thing your applicants will look for. It's also something a lot of managers create without much thought. If you think about your ideal candidate, does "Five years of experience in the field," really describe what you're looking for? What if you miss a superstar candidate who rose quickly in their last job over the course of just three years, or what if someone with ten years of experience decides the job is too junior?

Rather than pick an arbitrary amount of time, describe what you'd like your candidate to have learned from their experience. Write that your ideal candidate has a history of increasing responsibility in their company, or that they participated in a certain level of decision-making or that they have honed specific skills. That's really what you're getting at when you ask for a certain number of years' experience anyway.

Education is tricky too. Unless you're in academia or the position requires certain certifications or course work, carefully consider your educational requirements. Does your candidate absolutely need a bachelor's degree? Which is more important, a college degree or work experience?

There's some discussion these days about whether college adds much to one's ability to perform on the job. Does it really make a difference for your open position? Or, as with experience, would you be better off describing the kinds of things you want your applicant to know, regardless of whether it was learned at a university or on the job?

I've known plenty of excellent, experienced, sophisticated finance people who don't have master's degrees. You'd be very lucky to get them in your company, but that won't happen if your job description says you only want MBAs.

If instead, you say you want someone who's been through mergers or handled large real estate transactions or who's well-versed in governance, you're likely to get more applicants who have the skills and experience you need.

Of course, you need to consider the other people on your team. If they all have advanced degrees, a new hire without a comparable education might have a hard time getting their respect. But you can find that out during the interview process, which we'll cover ahead.

By the way, education is no guarantee of skill, though sometimes people think so. Once when I was a director at one of my companies (after more than a decade managing teams) a co-worker handed me a resume from one of his friends. This guy had recently completed his MBA at a prestigious university and was looking for work. He had no relevant work experience, but his cover letter said he was looking for a director or VP position.

As you might guess, I didn't hire him. Bringing a novice on to a team of experienced high performers, particularly with a better title than theirs, would have been a disaster for the team's morale as well as this kid's career. Regardless of his degree, there's not a chance he would have been successful. I really hope he came to his senses and got a job at a lower level that gave him time to learn the business.

Chapter 19: Activate Your Network

Career paths are never straight lines. Careers are built on a series of unpredictable events. A random meeting, a LinkedIn connection or an unexpected referral can all lead to a new job. In fact, in my experience, any of these is far more likely to connect you with your next boss than a resume sent to an HR department.

My career path looks like this:

- Applied to a job listing, but with an inside contact who walked my application in
- Recruited by someone I didn't know but who'd heard about me from someone else
- Promoted
- Recruited by someone I met at an industry event
- Referred by a former co-worker
- Referred by a business contact
- Recommended by a consultant
- Hired again by a former boss working at a new company
- Referred to a recruiter by a friend
- Introduced by a business contact
- Promoted
- Recruited by a LinkedIn contact
- Recruited by a business contact

In a couple of cases I not only changed jobs, but I also changed industries, so the network I'd developed for one industry wasn't as useful in the new one. But even then, it was contacts rather than established processes that worked in my favor.

And here's how I found the people I brought onto my teams (in order of frequency):

- Hired from within the company
- Hired based on referrals from my contacts
- Re-hired people I'd worked with in the past
- Hired from a company intern program
- Found via jobs sites/Craigslist/HR
- Discovered on trade organization job sites

You never know where your next great hire will come from. It might be someone who cold-called you six months ago or someone you met at a conference or a friend of a friend. In order to find those candidates, you can't just place an ad and hope for the best. You need to get the word out that you have an opening and that you have a great team.

Exactly how you do this will vary somewhat by industry. If you are looking for part-time employees or students or if you have mostly entry-level or unskilled positions, job sites may be perfect for you. People early in their careers don't have a well-developed network, so being highly visible online is the way to go, and your ad and job description will be critical in making the right first impression.

Of course, you'll also want to get the word out to schools, rec centers, coffee shops and other places your potential applicants might hang out.

But even if you're looking for seasoned people and the likelihood of finding your hire online is slim, you still have to post to job sites, and you have to pay attention to the results. While I didn't get a lot of people from online applications compared with other sources, I did get some excellent team members from them, and wading through the large number of applications was well worth my time, though it was a pain.

Once you've posted your opening, get the word out to people inside your company, your business contacts, trade organizations, professional groups, vendors, consultants, and social media connections. Give your next hire every opportunity to hear about your open position from every possible source.

One good source of referrals is your team. People who work for you have some skin in the game when they recommend an acquaintance. They know this person's performance will reflect on them too, so they're likely to refer people they genuinely believe will do a good job.

Make sure your team has the job description so they can pass it on. Maybe even consider a small gift for employees when they refer a candidate who then gets the job, if your company doesn't already offer referral bonuses.

Another source of good candidates is your own company. Hiring from within increases the chances that you're getting a great team member, and it comes with a lot of advantages. Their current manager may give you insights that will help you understand how well an applicant will fit on your team. You may have access to HR records, and lots of people in the company will be able to talk to you about working with this person.

Reputations go both ways. Just like you can check out internal applicants, the applicants can check you out too. They will discover your reputation, they will talk to your people about what it's like to work for you and they will decide whether they want to consider being on your team.

If you're a jerk manager, that decision will be easy.

If your people believe you are helping them succeed, that you have your focus on the business and that your ego doesn't get in your way, they will respect you and they will say good things about you to everyone, including potential applicants. Then when you have openings, you're more likely to get good internal candidates, and you are more likely to get good referrals from your team members' networks.

Vendors, suppliers, and contractors can be surprisingly good sources of applicants. These are people who know what's going on in your industry and at your competitors. Just as they have come to know you, they know lots of people who work in related or competing companies and they can discretely mention that you have an opening. More than once, I've had vendors approach me and ask if I was aware of an opening at a competitor.

Just be a bit cautious. Vendors and suppliers have an interest in placing people who will continue to use their services, so thoroughly research the applicants that come to you through them, but don't hesitate to include them in your outreach.

Depending on your industry, trade organizations may have sections of their websites devoted to job and resume postings. The good thing about finding people through trade organizations is that they are usually pretty engaged in your industry—after all, they are involved with the trade group.

Then, depending on your personal social media policy, let your followers know you have an opening. LinkedIn is an obvious place for this, but your personal Facebook page may not be. Do what makes sense for you, and what will make the best impression on a potential applicant.

Make sure your company has a great website that does a good job promoting the company's culture and, if possible, your team. If your company does a lot of hiring, there should be a "Careers" section where applicants can find job descriptions and apply. At the very least, have an email address for applicants to send in resumes.

If you do have a Careers section on your site, make sure prospective employees can read about what it's like to work at the company and consider including testimonials from current employees. Include videos showing the workplace and highlight things that would be attractive to applicants.

Check out your company's profile on Glassdoor and make sure there aren't any potential gotchas. If there are, be prepared to talk about them during the interview process if your candidate brings them up.

And make sure your outreach identifies candidates who may be a little harder to discover. Not every candidate will be savvy about looking for work, so they may not make it into the usual funnels. Make certain you are reaching people in all kinds of communities and from all kinds of cultures.

Finally, always remember this: whenever you talk to anyone about your opening, you're selling. You're selling the company, your team and yourself. If you want to make the best possible hire, you want to look like the best possible place to work.

When everything goes right, you will be as excited about your new hire as they will be about joining your team.

Chapter 20: Making the First Cut

"Hiring people is an art, not a science, and resumes can't tell you whether someone will fit into a company's culture."
Howard Schultz, former CEO of Starbucks

Now that the word is out about your opening and you're getting applications, your role changes. You go from salesperson to detective, and your job now is to look at resumes and applications, read between the lines and try to figure out which applicants have the basic skills you need.

Remember that these people have applied for your position based on what they've read in the job description. Unless you're overwhelmed with responses and need an excuse to disqualify people, give them a little wiggle room if they don't exactly match the requirements you listed. Maybe skills in one area offset minor deficiencies in another.

In fact, it's possible to find a candidate who brings something to the job that you didn't even know you needed. This is particularly true if your industry is undergoing a lot of change.

In one of my jobs, technology was rapidly altering the way we were doing business. For decades, there had been a clear line between people with creative skills and people with technical talents. We needed both, and those groups had clearly defined roles that never overlapped. But as software started replacing specialized equipment, I started seeing applicants for creative positions who also had computer expertise.

That was quite new. Most of us hadn't yet figured out how we would staff for the evolving business, but some of the creative people applying for my jobs were betting that technical skills would be important.

My job descriptions for creative roles didn't list technical expertise as a requirement (outside of basic creative tools), but once I noticed this new trend in my applicants, I began to understand how they might enable us to change the way we worked. With this new skill set, the old walls might come down, creative people might play a more technical role and technical people might flex their creative muscles.

And that's exactly how things eventually turned out: the creative folks merged with the technical people and we ended up with one team capable of filling many roles. There were still some differences in skills, but it was a much more flexible workforce. How lucky I was to learn from my applicants and, once they were hired, to work with them to figure out the best way to operate in our new environment.

If I had only considered applicants who had the job skills I *thought* I needed, I'd never have hired people with the skills I *really* needed. Even interviewing and hiring can lead to learning for managers who are paying attention.

All that said, your HR department may help weed out unqualified applicants, but since they don't know your team or its work as well as you do, make sure they really understand what you need and where you might be willing to give on the requirements. You don't want them to toss out a good candidate because they weren't a perfect match with the job description.

Once you have a batch of qualified applicants, pause for a moment and think about your timeline. When would you like someone to start? Working backward, how much notice will they give their current employer? Before that, how long for the background check or drug screen? And before that, how long will it take you to get them an offer letter? Then back some more—how long will negotiations take?

All that starts once your interview process ends and you are ready to make an offer. It's really important for you to understand how long this will all take, and it's equally important for you to set expectations with your applicants. Nothing is more confusing to an applicant than to have an employer show interest then suddenly go silent. Make sure your applicant knows what to expect and make sure you stay on that timeline or communicate any changes. Your future employee will form an impression of you during this process, so be sure to treat them with respect.

Check Them Out: References

Your detective work continues once you have a batch of finalists. Now it's time to contact them, do an initial phone interview and, assuming that goes well, ask for references. If they already provided references on the application, make sure you have at least one former manager on the list and if not, ask for one. It's completely understandable that an applicant might not want you to contact their current employer, but you want to talk with someone who managed them in the past. Co-workers can provide valuable information, but only a manager will know how this person really performed and how they worked as part of a team.

And here's the one place I will encourage you to bend a rule.

Most large companies have a policy about providing references. The policy usually goes something like this: Don't do it.

Companies instruct their managers to handle references by providing the dates of employment and the job title and nothing more.

They fear that by providing anything more, they will be liable. If they say something bad that prevents someone from getting a job, they will be liable for causing harm to the spurned applicant. If they say something good that encourages an employer to make a hire and things don't work out, they will be liable for misleading that company into making a bad choice.

These things may have happened before, though I've not heard of any examples. But if you follow this policy, you completely mess with the system. Why bother leaving on good terms if your manager can't say anything about it to a future employer? Why bother asking applicants for references if they aren't allowed to tell you anything anyway? The reason people build networks and use them to find jobs and candidates, and the reason it works, is that, for the most part, people find ways around this policy.

I'm sure many attorneys would disagree, so if you are worried about it, get creative. I once called an applicant's former supervisor to get a reference and was routed immediately to HR. I had hoped for an honest discussion, but now expected nothing more than the usual bland start-date-end-date-job-title-business from HR. And I did get those stats, but I also got another bit of information that bypassed the no-reference policy: this employee, the HR person said, is eligible for re-hire.

And that told me quite a lot. She did well; they liked her, and they'd welcome her back. I'd love more detail, and I'd love to be able to ask specific questions, but I'll take that endorsement any day.

Finally, set up a phone call or Zoom interview and speak to your finalists. Ask them about their previous work experience, their accomplishments, the things they're proudest of, the relationships they had with co-workers, what they enjoy most about their career. Ask why they've applied for this job and what they hope to get out of their next position. Listen carefully and gauge the honesty of the answers. Try to imagine whether they have the right demeanor for the team.

And of course, sell. Talk about what you like about the company and about your team. Talk about what you think the company is doing well and why it has a bright future. Come up with some stories you can tell that show what it's like to work on your team. Talk a bit about your work history—not in a boastful manner, just to provide some context for your current perspectives. Chances are your applicants have already checked out your LinkedIn profile, so don't go into too much detail.

At this stage, make sure you and your candidate are in the same salary and benefits ballpark. It's tricky to talk about money, so ask them if they are aware of the compensation package and see what they say. If they say they are not aware of it, provide the salary range and talk briefly about what determines where a candidate will be in that range. Does it depend on experience or some kind of quantifiable accomplishments? Your candidate will want to be at the top of the range, so be careful to set expectations appropriately.

Be aware that there is also a list of things you cannot talk about. You cannot ask about marital status, religion and a number of other things. These vary by state, so check with HR prior to doing this screening call to make sure you know the rules.

When you're done, let your candidate know about the next steps and your timeline. Where are you in the hiring process? When do you anticipate deciding who comes in for interviews? Be sure to stick to this timeline, and if things change, be sure to let your candidate know.

I don't have any "gotcha" questions, but I do like to end this screening interview by asking if there is anything we haven't covered that they think I should know. It's OK if they don't have anything to add, but if there's anything they haven't told you, this gives them that opportunity. I've heard some interesting, revealing things by asking this sort of open-ended question.

Chapter 21: Meet Your Next Employee

Now that you have a short list of people who fit your job description, whose references have been positive and who are generally aware of the compensation package, it's time to meet a select few of them face to face.

I think interviews should involve many people, for two reasons. First, you want to get a lot of points of view, and the more folks who meet your candidate, the more support you'll get for that hire. Second, you want your candidate to get a well-rounded sense of the atmosphere and the culture.

Jerk managers often feel like this is unnecessary, that they have the final say, so input from others isn't going to make a difference. They couldn't be more wrong.

It's very important for people on your team to meet their potential co-workers. More than anyone, they know what it's like to work on that team, and they can answer very specific questions. Also, you want to hear their thoughts about the candidate afterward. Interviewing someone who will be your peer yields completely different results than interviewing someone who will be your employee, and you want that information. Plus, the more buy-in you get at this stage from your team, the easier it will be for your new hire to assimilate after they start.

In very competitive markets, you may need to work hard to woo your top candidates. Think about things you can do to make an unusually good first impression during the interview. One small company I know flew their top candidate in for an interview and greeted her with a box of business cards printed with her name and title. They wanted to show how excited they were to have her join the company and to enable her to picture herself there. They also took team pictures that included her and sent her copies as part of the interview follow up. They did everything they could to make her feel like one of the team that day, and she ended up taking the job.

As you plan the interview, here are the things you should consider:

- Who from your team will make a good impression? How will you structure peer interviews? Group meeting or one-on-ones? Be sure to brief your group in advance by reminding them their job is to scrutinize but also to sell. Give the team copies of the applicants' resumes in advance. Be sure they know what topics are off-limits in job interviews.

- Should you introduce your candidate to your boss or to some of your peers? That depends on the level of the position and whether they will work with them after they are hired. Talk to your boss about the amount of involvement they'd like to have.

- Should your candidate talk with someone in HR? I think that's a very good idea.

Be sure to structure the day so that nothing unexpected happens. People should know when and where they are meeting your candidate and your candidate should know in advance who they'll be meeting. Remember, your candidate is forming an opinion of you and the company, so you want this to be a well-organized and positive experience all around.

Build in time for a tour of the offices or facilities and point out noteworthy things. Is there an interesting bit of architecture, a place where something historic happened, an awards display, an exceptionally nice lunchroom? As you give the tour, you'll be showing your pride in the company and its history and reputation.

Should the interview include breakfast or lunch? If so, who should attend? I think you should be the first one to meet your candidate and you should do that alone, so if you set up a breakfast, make it only with you. Lunch with the team might be a nice way to conduct a less formal group interview, assuming your people can take that kind of time and your expense budget allows for sandwiches.

You don't need to be present for all of this. You should be the first person your candidate sees and, if possible, you should ferry them from meeting to meeting, but you shouldn't be in every meeting. After all, you want your team to sing your praises, and that would be awkward with you in the room.

When it's your turn to have one-on-one time with your candidate, your goal will be to fill in any gaps and sell them on the company and on you. By now, you know them pretty well. You've seen their resume, you've talked to their references and you've had an initial phone interview, so this is your chance to picture them on your team and imagine how they might fit.

I sometimes like to ask what their process will be if we make an offer. I'm curious to know how they will treat their current employer. Will they feel obligated to give more than two weeks' notice? Will they leave as soon as the offer is extended? I like to see that my candidate thinks about the impact their leaving will have. That tells me they feel they make an important contribution, and they care about their company enough to allow time to adjust to their departure.

When it's all over, you should be the last person your candidate sees. Get their impressions of the team and the company. See if they have any last questions for you and let them know your next steps and your timeline. (Then remember to let your applicants know if your timeline changes. You don't want your top candidates to think you've changed your mind if things don't happen according to the schedule you set.)

Then go back and talk to the people who met your candidate and get their impressions. If your team met as a group, get them back together briefly and ask them for their thoughts. It's not important for you to talk about how you feel at this stage—you obviously liked this candidate well enough to bring them in—this is a time for you to listen.

And finally, once all your finalists have gone through the interview process and you have gathered the feedback from your team, you need to make the call. Decide on your top candidate and get ready to pick up the phone. It's time to negotiate.

Chapter 22: Offer and Negotiation

Before you make an offer to a prospective employee, be ready to answer questions about a few very important things:

- Know your benefits package in detail, including health, dental and vision insurance (and the portion paid by the employee), vacation, sick and personal time policies, federal and state holidays observed, life and other insurance options, 401k and company match, etc. Have all this information at your fingertips. It's all part of the compensation package and may be very persuasive.

- Understand how bonuses work and the factors that determine the amount an employee will receive—are there external factors out of the employee's direct control?

- Know what perks come with this job—car allowance, parking spot, public transit discounts, free coffee, free lunches, pets in the office, etc.

- Are there fixed hours or are the hours flexible? Do you allow remote work?

- What is the process for salary increases? Are they scheduled and are they tied to performance?

- And finally, understand your autonomy in deciding what to offer. Do you need to check with anyone before quoting a salary if it exceeds a certain amount or can you wrap this up during the call?

Also, make sure your timeline is completely buttoned up. If you make an offer and it's accepted, what comes next and when? In my experience, here's what to expect:

- Day 1 – offer made
- Day 2 – offer accepted
- Day 4 – offer letter sent

- Day 5 – offer letter returned, signed
- Day 6 – background check and drug screen scheduled
- Day 8 – drug screen appointment
- Day 11 – results of the background check and drug screen
- Day 12 – notification to employee and determination of start date (employee gives notice to current employer)
- Days 26-33 – first day in the office

Assuming your company has a similar process, it's a month from the moment you made the offer until your new employee walks in the door! And that timeline can easily increase if the employee takes a couple of days to review the offer or wants to take a vacation between jobs. All the more reason you want to fill open positions quickly.

Note that you don't leave your other candidates hanging this whole time. Let them know you're still in progress on the position and when they can expect to hear from you. After all, if things go awry with your first selection, you want the next in line to still feel good about the company, so keep everyone in the loop.

OK, now that you have your benefits information and your timeline in order, it's time for that call.

I like to start by telling my top candidate how much we all enjoyed meeting them during the interview process and that we'd like to make an offer. I then run through a high-level summary of the benefits package and perks, mentioning the bonus if there is one but staying away from the numbers. Then I ask my candidate what salary they had in mind. I really don't like to throw out the first number. You may have already discussed the salary range, so the question should be where in that range should this person start.

When you hear their number, if it's out of line say so and counter with your number. If you can accept their number, do so without further negotiation. Don't let your ego get in the way. This isn't about winning, it's about bringing someone on to your team at a fair salary. Law of Management #5 reminds us that *The Person with the Smallest Ego Wins*, so when the salary is fair, don't keep negotiating just so you can come out on top. You have a great candidate who is going to feel great about this negotiation, so you've already won.

146

Once I offered a job to a candidate and asked him to give me his salary requirement. He gave me a number that happened to match mine exactly. I said, "Done," and we started talking about a start date. Years later, after we'd both gone our separate ways, he told me that experience was one of the things that really motivated him in that job. He had expected to be ground down during the salary negotiation because that's how he'd always been treated, and my quick acceptance of his first number made him feel respected and needed. And he was a great hire. Even during tough times, he always performed at the highest level and had a great attitude. I think some of that has to be because we got off to a great start.

When you're negotiating a salary, it's yet another good time for you to remember Law of Management #3: *Everyone Knows Everything.* Arrive at a fair salary that's in line with the rest of the team and all will be well when word gets out. Underpaying will make your new hire feel like a fool for accepting such a low number and overpaying will make everyone else on the team angry.

I once had a great candidate who was making an industry change. He was coming from an industry notorious for low pay to one that was quite generous. Unfortunately, we never had a salary range discussion during the interview process, so when I offered him the job and asked him how much he wanted, he gave me a number that was a little more than half of what I was willing to pay.

I could have accepted it, and he'd have been perfectly happy for a while. But when he eventually found out he was severely underpaid I have no doubt I would have lost a great employee. He either would have left in anger or become a very disgruntled guy, and one not very happy with me. Once a salary is set, it's nearly impossible in most companies to make big corrections, so even if I had a change of heart and tried to bump him up, he'd be underpaid for years.

So instead of accepting his number, I offered him mine, which was almost double his. From day one, he was a happy, top-performing model employee, and his positive attitude rubbed off on the rest of the team. Talk about getting off on the right foot. It would have been a disaster to trade all that for some savings in payroll.

Like everything else you do, negotiating with a job candidate must be done in a way that benefits the company the most. Making them feel like they've been treated fairly sets them up to be happy, productive employees, which is exactly what the company deserves.

Maybe you can't agree on salary. At this point, you may be tempted to stretch a bit and go for a higher number just to wrap this up. After all, you have invested so much time and energy into this candidate already, and you really need to fill the vacancy, so you don't want to start over. But before you do, ask yourself what will happen to the rest of the team when they find out. An unproven newcomer making that much might really set them off. Once that happens, any benefit to saving a few days in the hiring process will be lost and you'll have a tough time undoing the damage you've done to the team. It could take years to rebuild trust, and the new team member will have a hard time fitting in. It's much better to move on to your next candidate than to make an exception that spoils the team.

One word of caution: be absolutely certain that you can keep any promises you make during the hiring process, even ones that aren't exactly commitments but are, let's say, optimistic views of the future. If you suggest there will be a salary bump after three months, there needs to be one. If you say a 5% increase is likely after a year, it must happen. If you don't keep your promises (or your confidently worded predictions) you may have a legal problem on your hands, and you will certainly have an employee who feels like you cheated them.

And finally, as soon as your candidate has a start date, get back to all the applicants you corresponded with who didn't get the job and let them know. Unfortunately, this courtesy has become very rare, but I believe it's important to let each person you wrote to or spoke with know that you filled the job. Though they will be disappointed, they will appreciate that you aren't leaving them hanging. And you never know what the future holds. One of these people may be perfect for another opening down the road or they may one day become your boss.

Never miss an opportunity to make a good impression because you just never know.

Chapter 23: Avoiding Discrimination

There are lots of laws and policies regarding discrimination in the workplace. You should know and follow them at all times. Even if you think you know all the laws, review them periodically just to keep it top of mind.

But avoiding discrimination shouldn't be difficult. You shouldn't have to be on your guard all the time. You should simply behave in a way that never gets you in trouble in the first place.

You have a responsibility to hire people with the right skills, encourage good performance and reward them based on merit. That means preventing irrelevant things from influencing your judgment and affecting the work environment. In other words, avoiding discrimination.

Hiring Discrimination

Few things you do as a manager are as tightly regulated as hiring. For very good reasons, there are lots of rules about what questions you can and cannot ask during interviews, and what criteria you can and cannot use when selecting your top candidate.

Before you start the hiring process, make sure you know all the rules in your state and city and make sure you are aware of your company's policies around hiring. This book has none of that information, so be sure to get it from your HR folks and make sure you understand it thoroughly.

But there is some practical advice that will help both to keep you out of trouble and get the right person in the door.

First, you need to stay focused on the job. Take a good, objective look at the job description for your open position. Depending on the job, you may want a candidate with specific experiences. You may want certain skills. You absolutely want the best candidate for the job.

But does it matter whether they're married? Does their age matter? Does their skin color have any impact on the requirements in the job description? Does this job require employees to be a specific gender?

If you focus purely on the job requirements, does any of this matter? No, it doesn't.

The job requirements are your only criteria. None of these other factors will prevent an applicant from qualifying or from performing well. If you think otherwise, you're exposing biases that have nothing to do with the job.

But, you may think, a woman may want to take time off to have kids. An older applicant may struggle with technology. Only a man is physically strong enough.

Of course, this is all nonsense.

I've known many highly accomplished, extremely talented women with children who never shorted their jobs for a second and whose companies valued them highly and rewarded them extremely well.

I've known older software engineers who could code circles around their younger counterparts. I have a friend nearing 70 who is one of the top software engineers at one of the largest tech companies in the world.

I've known incredibly successful people of all races and genders and religions with various sexual orientations, body types, hairstyles, tattoos and lifestyles. If you focus on the job and ignore irrelevant secondary factors, you'll hire the most talented person available.

Leave your personal biases out of it and nothing except a person's qualifications and abilities will prevent them from meeting the requirements of the job.

But you may still think, you need to make sure this next hire is a good fit for the team. I don't think my team would welcome a woman/Latinx/50-year-old/whatever.

More nonsense, for two reasons. First, you are making assumptions about your team that may not be correct. Second, if your assumptions are correct, data suggests you will improve the performance of your team if you bring in these new perspectives and work with your team to accept them.

Study after study shows that companies with gender and cultural diversity are more profitable than companies that are relatively homogeneous. Building an inclusive team is the right thing to do for your company. It will make your team stronger and your company more successful. And if you focus on what's really important for each opening, you will do just that.

Also, as your company's recruiting and hiring policies will certainly remind you, it's against the law to do anything else.

Workplace Discrimination

Rules about discrimination in the workplace can get very specific. There's a long list of things you cannot say or do and several categories of employees who are legally protected. Of course, you must know these rules, but I've found that if you follow only this one, you will stay out of hot water: *never think, do, or say anything that would make a member of your team feel different from the rest of the group.*

You may not intend to be derogatory, discriminatory or inappropriate, but simply pointing out something that sets someone apart from the rest of the group exposes your biases and damages the group's cohesion. Even if you're attempting a compliment ("Women are better multitaskers") you've just singled out one person and highlighted something that makes them different.

And you've revealed something about yourself. What other things do you think are true about women? Simply by mentioning gender (or any other characteristic), you've let people know that's an issue for you. They'll be watching for more evidence of your bias from that moment on.

I've seen managers poke fun at team members for just about every reason imaginable: facial hair, gender, religion, ethnicity, stature, weight, gender, sexuality, everything. The response is nearly always the same: an uncomfortable chuckle and averted eyes.

Managers rarely intend to be insulting, but simply by pointing out a difference, they have shown the employee and the team that they think this person is not like the rest. In an attempt to be funny, these managers can reinforce painful stereotypes that people have been trying to overcome for generations. And they've done nothing to move the company forward.

Your job is not to be funny. First, it's to get the best work out of your team. Second, it's to behave in a way that doesn't make you a lawsuit magnet.

Be aware that you can have a hostile work environment without the existence of obvious victims. People who are insulted or offended don't always act like it. Sometimes they will play along, laugh and even join in, in a self-deprecating way. That's defensive behavior. It's how

151

some employees try to defuse an unpleasant conversation. They're not enjoying themselves in the least. It's your job to notice and prevent the behavior that's making them uncomfortable and damaging the cohesion of your team.

Good team dynamics depend on trust and cohesion, and the understanding that everyone shares a common goal and is working with equal effort to achieve it. Separating someone from the rest of the team by mentioning irrelevant characteristics can damage this cohesion.

Set a good example, then don't tolerate poor behavior from your team. Make it clear from the outset that there is no room for behavior that sets some team members apart from the rest. Respond quickly if you see folks behaving inappropriately. Don't be surprised if at first they are shocked that you'd think them racist or ageist or sexist. But help them understand that what they intended as fun was actually harmful and destructive and has no place on your team. After all, creating or allowing a hostile work environment can be grounds for dismissal.

Chapter 24: The First Day

You've worked hard to make a good impression on your candidate during the interview process. Now, make a great impression on your new employee on their first day at work.

By the time your employee arrives, everything they need to get started should be ready. Remember the hiring timeline—you've had two to three weeks to prepare for this moment, so there's no excuse for not being completely ready.

If your employee needs a laptop, it should be ready to go. If they need business cards, they should be printed. There should be a place for your new hire to sit, and if you use nameplates in your office, theirs should be in place. If you use photo IDs, make an appointment for your new hire to get their picture taken. If you have an orientation process, make an appointment for that too.

Know what the HR policies are for new hires and make sure everything that needs to be done is done in a timely way. Sometimes there are training videos or company policy reviews that new employees should see. This day should be as organized and seamless as the interview day was.

Assign someone on your team to help your new hire for their first few days. This person should take them to lunch on their first day and accompany them to any team meetings or other activities.

Depending on the level of their position, consider walking your new employee around to meet your management team peers and your boss. Your employee will feel important, and hopefully, your peers will remember their name and say hello in the hallway later.

It's amazing to me how often companies drop the ball once they've made a job offer. They seem surprised that the employee needs a laptop or business cards, so the process of getting those things together doesn't even start until the new hire has arrived.

Smart companies focus on amazing first-day experiences. One company takes new employees out to lunch, has them build their own ergonomically correct chair and ends the day with drinks. Others have a complete schedule of meetings with payroll, HR and the CEO.

Whatever your process, your new employee should end their first day feeling lucky to be there. They should see that you cared enough to ease their transition into the company. They will know people, they'll be squared away with HR and payroll and they will repay you with trust, loyalty and hard work.

On my first day in one of my jobs, I waited in the lobby for quite a while until my boss's assistant finally came to get me. Then I spent five minutes with the boss, was pointed in the general direction of my office and dismissed. That was it. I'd not been introduced to any of my peers nor had a tour of the building during the interview, and I wasn't about to get any of that now.

I spent my first day wandering around, finding my management team peers and introducing myself. That company made a lousy first impression on me, and in many ways, they never recovered.

While the following days don't need to be as tightly orchestrated, continue to do things to help your new hire settle in. Ask them if they'd be comfortable talking about themselves a bit at their first staff meeting. Think of opportunities to introduce them to more people and help them take advantage of company programs or perks.

Give them advice that will help them succeed. I once started a new job that required me to spend a lot of time with another team in the company. My boss gave me great advice: she said whenever you are in the room with that team's manager, laugh at his jokes. At first, I thought she was kidding, but she assured me she wasn't. So, I did my best. And after my first meeting with that manager, he came into my boss's office and congratulated her on making such a great hire.

Things Nobody Will Tell You
Saving Money Can Be Expensive

Some companies are overzealous about pinching pennies, and it costs them dearly.

If you want to boost morale, inspire hard work and build loyalty to the company, spend $20 on bagels now and then. When someone's chair breaks, spend $100 to fix it. If you have a crew working on Thanksgiving, have a turkey and trimmings delivered to the workplace.

These inexpensive but thoughtful things make employees feel appreciated, and they will repay you many times over. Your return on those little investments will take the form of a few extra hours of work, willingness to come in early or stay late to work on a special project, declining an offer from a competitor—all benefits to the company that are far more valuable than the few dollars it costs to be thoughtful.

On the other hand, if you want to turn your employees into malcontents, tell them there's no budget for sandwiches when you need them to work over their lunch. Tell them you don't have money for chair repairs, so just put a little duct tape on it (this actually happened!) or tell them their thanks for working holidays is the state-mandated holiday pay. The losses in turnover and angry employees extracting every penny they can in overtime and reimbursements will be far greater than the cost of a tray of sandwiches from Subway or a roasted turkey from the grocery store.

Chapter 25: When Good Hires Go Bad

All hires are good hires. After all, nobody sets out to make a bad hire. But sometimes, things don't work out. And that's not necessarily a reflection on the employee, nor is it always a reflection on you.

I've never met anyone who doesn't *care* about work. I've known plenty of people who didn't like their jobs or their managers or even their companies, but that's not the same as not caring. In fact, you must care about something in order to dislike it—if you don't care, you'll feel nothing. Work is too much a part of our identities for us not to care.

But people can be in the wrong job. Sometimes the truth is the job and the employee are not a good fit. That employee might be great in another role, but they are failing in this one. I've let people go who went on to be very successful even though they were not at all successful on my team. The job and the employee need to fit, and when they don't, it's up to you to make a change.

Letting people go can be painful and legally tricky, and can throw your entire team into turmoil. Or it can be a few difficult conversations for you and—eventually—a positive experience for those who remain.

This chapter helps managers do the right thing at each step of a difficult process that is both emotional and rewarding.

People know who the poor performers are on their team. Even when a poor performer is well-liked, team members and often people outside the organization can see what's going on. Keeping that person on the team creates problems for those who have to compensate for their poor work.

Team members who take pride in their work are offended by a peer who doesn't carry their weight. Their confidence in the company is shaken. After all, if the company doesn't know enough about the team to identify a low performer, how can they possibly know about the top performers? Can the company even tell them apart?

Low performers not only drag the team down and create extra work for everyone else, they lower morale. And if you don't deal with them, you will look like an ineffective manager who can't make a difficult decision for the good of the team and the company. You need to solve this problem.

This is a good place for a reminder that your HR folks will be helpful here and must be in the loop. They need to know when you have a performance problem on your team, and they can help you follow policies designed to keep you and the company out of trouble.

One thing you should ask yourself is whether you (and the company you represent) have done everything you can to help this person succeed. Talk to your low performer and let them know that you are aware they are not performing up to par. Give them a chance to explain their perspective and listen thoroughly.

Then consider whether there are any internal obstacles to their success. Internal obstacles are things like workplace discrimination, lack of training, or bullying. You can do something about those, and you must. It would be a shame to lose a potentially valuable employee because of team dysfunction, and if it happens once, it will happen again.

On the other hand, some external obstacles, like trouble in a marriage or financial problems, must be managed by the employee. You have no right nor obligation to get involved in these personal problems, but you do have an obligation to keep them from getting in the way of your team's success. If your company has some type of employee assistance program, encourage this person to take advantage of it, but keep up your efforts to improve the performance or move the employee out.

Once you've concluded that there are no external obstacles to your employee's success, it's time to put your employee on a performance improvement plan, or "PIP."

The PIP accomplishes one of two things: it either helps your employee improve their performance so that it rises to the level of rest of the team, or it creates the justification for their dismissal and documents your efforts.

Does your troubled employee understand the job requirements? Do they know how their performance is being measured? There are several correctable reasons that an employee might fail, and the PIP is designed to expose those reasons while tracking your efforts to help them. Should you find yourself in a wrongful dismissal dispute, you'll need to show you did everything you could and the PIP, along with communication around its use, is a big part of that.

The PIP will:

- Describe the performance issues that are not acceptable
- Clearly communicate the expectations of the job
- Clearly state things the employee needs to do to improve
- Set measurable goals to determine whether the improvements are happening
- Set a timetable for achieving the goals
- State the consequences if the goals are not met

Once you fill out the PIP, which you should do with your HR folks, it's time to present it to your underperformer.

These are some of the most difficult discussions you will have. You need to tell this person they are not up to par, where they are coming up short and what they need to do to improve. You need to help them understand you will be supportive of them through this process, but that there will be consequences if they don't take it seriously.

Present the PIP and walk through each step. Listen to the employee as they describe their view of the goals and timetable. You may still learn something you didn't know that prompts you to make revisions. Or, as with an overly defensive employee, you may simply confirm the decision to put this person on a PIP in the first place.

After you've gone through the PIP, have the employee sign it, indicating that they have read and understood it, whether or not they agree with it. Then give them a copy of the PIP so they can get to work. If an employee refuses to have the conversation or refuses to accept and sign the PIP, you may be able to consider that failure to pass the PIP and move forward with dismissal. Your HR people will guide you through that.

Once the PIP is in place, it's now your job to follow the plan. Evaluate and chart the employee's progress, and let them know how they're doing. Encourage them, but be honest when they are in danger of missing milestones or not achieving their performance goals. Communicate thoroughly throughout the process but particularly when milestones arrive. Congratulate them on any progress and make sure they know it must continue as they follow the plan to its conclusion. Or let them know they are not succeeding. Always communicate in email, and save the emails to document your communication. Summarize any verbal discussions you have in an email to the employee immediately, then send a copy to HR.

Throughout this process, remember that the PIP is designed to give the employee every opportunity to make things right, so make sure your attitude reflects that too.

Often an underperforming employee will voluntarily leave the company during the PIP process. The PIP helps them to understand the work they need to do and that you are serious about moving them out if they can't do it, so they may decide to go on their own rather than suffer the embarrassment of being fired.

If the employee successfully completes the PIP, congratulations to you. You have turned around a poor performer. Now it will be up to both of you to make sure improvement continues so you can move beyond this rough patch.

If the employee fails to meet the goals of the PIP, it's time to let them go. Consult your HR people about any severance you might give and the process they'll have for dismissing an employee. Then once the employee is gone, meet with the team and let them know.

As always, don't say anything negative, even though the employee was a poor performer. You don't need to explain what went wrong or how you tried to help them improve. The team already knows everything they need to know. Just express your disappointment that this had to happen and that you'll move quickly to fill the vacancy. Remember, the person you let go may still have friends on the team so be sympathetic, both to the team and to the person who's gone no matter how bad their behavior might have been. You don't need inappropriate comments to get back to your angry former employee and their eager attorney.

Things Nobody Will Tell You
Tough Conversations Get Easier

The first time you sit down to have a difficult conversation with an employee, you'll be understandably nervous. Though you'll be well prepared and you'll probably be accompanied by someone from your HR team, you will still be conscious of the impact this discussion is having on your employee and, depending on how they react, you may feel quite bad. After all, look what you're doing to their career.

In a calmer moment, you'll realize that you're not doing anything to their career. They have put their career in jeopardy by not performing at the level their job demands. You are protecting your team. And once you've been through it a couple of times—sat calmly as people burst into tears or become outraged—it gets easier. Much easier. Keep your focus on the team and your job and the drama of these conversations will have little effect on you.

Part Three: Managing Your Career

Now that you're a great manager, you're working hard. You're keeping your ego in check, you're aware of your team's needs and you're inspiring them to live up to the brand you've established. You're managing your boss and your peers to prevent things from getting in your team's way but still, every day brings new challenges. You have a lot going on.

With everything else you're doing, it's hard to get a break from the constant work of managing your team and take a few minutes to think about yourself and your career.

You're tough, and you're successful. But now and then you need to take a little time for yourself. After all, great managers are some of a company's most valuable assets, so you need to make sure you are taking care of this one by maintaining your ability to perform at the highest level.

I'm not talking about pedicures, I'm talking about things you can do to give yourself a break from the day-to-day that will enrich your career and help you feel good about what you're doing.

Use Your Network

Your network is the term for the vast number of people you know. Some, but not all, will be people in your industry. Some will be peers at your company and competing companies, and some will be former employees and bosses. Your network will include vendors, suppliers, school friends and family. It will consist of people who will answer your text immediately and people who may not.

Your network provides you with many benefits. Some people in your network will be good collaborators, people who are good at brainstorming and bouncing ideas back and forth. Some will be good counselors who can listen as you describe challenges and provide helpful advice. Some will be people you talk to often, others you will contact sparingly.

A good network helps you maintain a good attitude because it's easy to feel alone when you're a manager and connecting with people in your network helps you realize you are part of a community of people who understand that.

You should let your network know when you have an opening on your team, and when you're looking for work. Find an appropriate, humble way to let certain people in your network know about your accomplishments, like when your team wins an award, or when you get promoted. Don't be boastful, just make sure the people who are pulling for you know that you and your team are succeeding.

A good network helps you maintain your skills because you can see how others are solving the problems you face. You can talk with people about how they manage their bosses, handle budget presentations and deal with difficult employees. Some people in your network will be jerk managers, but you will identify them quickly so you won't heed their bad advice. In fact, you may find opportunities to help other managers become better by mentoring them or at least by advising them to heed the Laws of Management.

And always remember, a network is made up of two-way streets. Just as you will get good advice and a sympathetic ear, you need to provide the same when people in your network are in need. Of course, you won't give away trade secrets, but you can still be helpful and supportive. Because you never know where your next opportunity will come from, who will be your next boss, or who might be the perfect hire.

Being a good citizen of your network means not abusing your contacts by trying to sell them something they don't need or becoming a nuisance rather than a collaborator. It means being a contributor by providing references and leads when people need them, offering advice and helping out when you are able.

And most of all, being a good network citizen means being honest and acting with integrity. Your network is a very effective tool that can help you in many ways, but it's also very efficient at getting the word out that you can't be trusted.

Avoid Burnout

Burnout is that feeling that nothing you do matters anymore. It's that overwhelming sense that you can't possibly keep up with everything so why bother trying?

Burnout can creep up on you. One day you can feel on top of the world, and the next you feel ground down and depressed. You feel powerless to fix the problems above you, and so it seems futile to try to fix the problems below.

In my experience, burnout is a sign that I need to make a change. Sometimes it's just changing the way I work. If I'm overwhelmed, is it because I'm not managing well? Should I be delegating more? Are my people empowered to do their jobs without checking in over and over? Am I afraid to leave early or take a day off because things will fall apart? Those are problems that lead to feelings of burnout, but they are also problems I can fix.

Is my boss constantly taking up my time, asking me questions or telling me what to do? Does my boss not feel like I have things under control? Are they getting input from someone else that things aren't going well? These are also things I can fix, or at least I can make a good attempt at it.

Am I constantly online evenings and weekends, checking messages and email, afraid to unplug for a few hours in case something important happens? Is this need real? Or am I a little bit of a micromanager who needs to step back and let the team do its work?

If you find you are the source of your own burnout, sit down and think about what exactly triggers those feelings and what you can do about it. Do you need to designate someone on your team as your second-in-command, someone who can step in when you're unavailable, who can give you peace of mind? Do you need to better communicate with your boss about your team's progress, to increase confidence that your group is on the right track?

The first way to combat burnout is to look at the things you can do to prevent it, then make it a priority to get those things done. Remember, until you started feeling burned out, you were one of the company's most important assets: a great manager. You owe it to your company to restore the value of that asset as quickly as you can.

Another way to combat burnout is to get away. Has it been four years since you've taken a vacation? Honestly, is that because the company has needed you every single day? Because you've built a needy team that can't operate without your constant involvement? Or do you think there is something valiant and honorable about foregoing vacations? After all, you've heard people boast about how long it's been since they took a vacation. But did you ever wonder what they're doing wrong to create that problem?

Not getting away for vacations or conferences or retreats makes your world feel smaller and smaller. You get into a rut, think the same thoughts, solve the same problems, deal with the same people. And if you thrive on building things, constant improvement and energizing your team, this sameness can feel like putting on a straitjacket every morning.

I believe you should take as much vacation as you earn. You owe it to your company to stay fresh and engaged. You owe it to your team to return with a new perspective on the business. And you owe it to yourself to find a fresh way of thinking about the product and to recharge.

One of my favorite bosses insisted I take vacation time, even though I insisted I didn't need it. Sure enough, after a week or two out of the office, I came back with new ideas about how to improve the business. When my mind wasn't forced to go through the routines of managing the daily grind, it was free to have new experiences and think of new approaches to our problems. For those few days, I went from being a manager to being a consumer, which led to new ways of seeing our product and gave me new ideas about how to serve our customers.

I didn't spend my vacation thinking about the product or the company. I took full advantage of the time off and tried to forget work as much as possible. But those thoughts crept into my consciousness anyway, so when I returned to work, I realized that the way I thought about the company and the product had evolved, and I was able to think of new ways of solving problems and innovating improvements.

No matter what your company does, it's easy to feel that all your customers care as passionately about your product as you do, that each consumer is aware of every nuance in the product, just like you are. It's natural and important for a company to focus on differentiation and product improvement, but it's equally natural that you lose your sense of how you fit into your customer's world when you do that.

Get away from the business for a while and you'll return with a much more realistic view of the product. You'll feel more connected to your customers. Your mind will be free to come up with ideas about how to improve things. And you'll have avoided becoming burned out.

Conferences and Workshops

Depending on your industry, there may be opportunities to attend conferences, seminars and workshops, to get additional training or just to see what trends are emerging and the kinds of work others are doing. You should take advantage of the best of these opportunities.

Trade associations often have the best conferences. Businesses can hold conferences as well, but those are often selling events more than they are learning opportunities. National trade groups often have local chapters. See what's available, reach out to your network to see which conferences the people you admire attend, then sign up and go.

There really is something to be said for getting away from the office for a couple of days, seeing how others work and getting a different perspective on your industry. As you advance in your career, you may also become a presenter, sharing your insights and discoveries with others.

Sometimes, it's difficult to convince your boss you need to dip into the travel budget for a conference, but it's worth the effort. Conferences offer exposure to new information and a chance to recharge your batteries and come back to work with new ideas and things you can share with your boss, peers and team. Do your best to explain the benefits of attending and find out how people in your network have convinced their bosses of the value of conferences.

Then once you've successfully got your boss to agree to let you go, come back with lots of positive reinforcement. Let them know about the new concepts you learned. Tell them about the people you met who might be candidates for future openings. Maybe even put together a presentation for the management team so everyone can see what a good investment the conference turned out to be.

If your trade organization gives out awards, be sure your team enters those contests. Nothing makes a conference seem worthwhile like coming back with an award the boss can brag about.

And use the networking opportunities that conferences provide. Spend some time with people from your network. A little face-to-face conversation is a great way to reinforce a relationship that relies on texts, posts, or phone calls the rest of the year.

Do your best to meet new people. The more people you know and who know you, the easier it will be to make your next great hire or get your next awesome job offer. Make the extra effort to go to receptions and breakfasts, attend break-out sessions, introduce yourself to interesting panelists or speakers. By now, you've developed the confidence you need to be a great manager, so that same confidence will enable you to introduce yourself to strangers at conferences. Don't be shy.

In between conferences, take advantage of seminars and workshops. There may be local events and online sessions that can inexpensively add to your knowledge, and offer a way to meet people you can add to your network. Don't hang back. Take part in Q&A sessions. In fact, asking a great question in front of a trade group audience can be a good way of getting your name out there and meeting people with similar points of view.

And after each webinar or workshop, be sure to provide your boss with a recap of what you learned. It's good to reinforce that you are always looking for ways to improve your knowledge and skills and that any money spent was a good investment.

Learn from Everyone

Every time your boss says something that makes you feel good, take a moment to think about what just happened. Was this a rare compliment from an ogre, a welcome but temporary relief? Or was this another exchange with the boss affirming that you and your team are on the right track? Do you spend the rest of the day walking on eggshells so you can hang on to this good feeling as long as possible? Or are you fired up to share the compliment with your team and inspire them to even greater heights?

And when the boss says something that makes you feel bad, think about that too. Was this yet another insult from a boss who can't see the good work your team is doing? Do you try to let it roll off your back because you know there's nothing you can do to prevent the next swipe anyway? Do you attempt to shield your team so they don't become demoralized too?

Or do you realize you've disappointed a boss who always has your back and wants the best for your team? Do you take the comments to heart, knowing they are meant to help, and work with your team to prevent a repeat?

In either case, you can learn from the exchange. By considering the nature of your conversations with the boss and the way you react, you can learn how to inspire your team and avoid demoralizing and demotivating your people.

You can also learn from your peers. In management team meetings, see how your fellow managers describe their teams and the work they do. Think about the brand they are building with their words and watch how the boss reacts to their comments. Your peers can provide examples, both positive and negative, of how to position teams and how to manage the boss.

As you get to know people from other teams in the company, you'll get a feel for how their managers operate, and you can compare that with what you see in the management meeting. Does a manager with an engaged, productive team promote them? Does a manager with an unhappy, disgruntled team throw them under the bus? Over time, you'll see examples of things that you will want to emulate and that you will want to avoid.

You can also learn from your employees. They are in the trenches every day, and by encouraging them to look for ways to improve their work, by being open when they come to you with suggestions, you will learn things you can use to make your team more successful and help your boss to appreciate their (and your) innovation.

Your team also has you as a boss, and they may see and experience things you don't intend. Even the best bosses sometimes send unintended messages or miss opportunities to provide support. Encourage your team to be open with you, but also watch their reactions closely. You may find that you have been unintentionally critical or ingenuously positive. You may find ways to refine your communication, to make sure what you intend to say is what your team ends up hearing.

Apply for Other Jobs

I once knew someone who would apply for jobs every few months even though she was perfectly happy where she was. She called it "checking my value," and she used it to determine her marketability and income potential. I don't know that I'd recommend that as a matter of course—eventually people will be onto you and they'll assume you're just testing the waters when they see your application—but if you see a job that appeals to you and that you would take under the right circumstances, apply for it, even if you're happy where you are. In my case, I try to change jobs every three or four years because I feel I have more opportunities to learn, grow and advance than if I stay in one position for longer than that. The only exception was a job that constantly offered new opportunities and new challenges, and that kept me engaged without having to look elsewhere.

Your industry or company may provide reasons to stay longer or leave earlier, so decide what's right for you, but don't let yourself stagnate in one spot for too long.

Applying for a job gives you a chance to update your resume, which by itself is an eye-opening experience. Because you're a great manager, chances are you can add several new accomplishments and maybe a promotion since the last time you looked at it.

Applying outside your company or business unit can also keep you from becoming complacent. Nothing keeps you on your toes and tests your skills like plunging into a new experience, forging your way with a new boss and a new team.

And the application process is useful too. It helps to see other company's job descriptions, to see what qualities they feel are important in their hires. If you have an interview, it will be interesting to see how you are treated, how the company positions itself and what they find interesting and valuable about you. And of course, it's always valuable to see what other companies pay and what their benefits are.

You do need to commit though. As you know from your own experience as a manager, you want to hire someone who really wants the job. You can sense lackluster enthusiasm from far away, and so can the person who is thinking about hiring you. Go after this job seriously or don't go after it at all.

Once you've committed, pull out all the stops. Arguably, the best time to look for work is when you're happy in your current position. You're not trying to leave a bad situation, so you won't appear bitter, and you're not unemployed so you won't look desperate.

If you get an offer, you have two great choices: stay where you are, where you are happy; or take the new job. However, be aware that the way you handle those choices can affect your reputation for a long

170

time to come. If you use the new job as leverage for a raise at the old one, neither your old boss nor your prospective new boss will be happy. Nobody likes being blackmailed and nobody likes being used. And if your boss calls your bluff, you have to leave whether you like it or not, which may not be the outcome you want.

If you decide to stay, there must be good reasons for turning down the offer, so be prepared to explain them. Remember, they have invested in you and asked you to join their company, so they deserve to know where they came up short if they ask.

If you take the new job, leave the old job in a gracious, classy way. Thank everybody and do right by them. Remember Law of Management #4, *You Are Not a Genius*, and acknowledge all the people who helped make you the success you have become.

If your company does formal exit interviews, think long and hard before being critical of your boss or of the company. Even if the interviewer promises anonymity, any negative comment you make will get out, and those are the kinds of things that can haunt you your entire career.

I have been hired by the same boss twice and I have been hired by the same company twice, and neither of those things would have happened had I not left happy and grateful and with a glowing exit interview.

Part Four: Thriving in the Real World

Now that you've made it to the end of this book, you have the perspective and tools you need to be a great manager and build a very successful career. You have developed a way to look at management that very few other people have, and it will set you apart from—and ahead of—your competition as you make your way up.

Throughout this book, you have learned the importance of keeping your ego under control. Keeping your ego in check may be a daily battle, even an hourly one. Nobody enjoys feeling insulted or disrespected whether those feelings are real or imagined, but reacting to these feelings will set you back and expose your weaknesses.

You've also seen the importance of earning respect by communicating frequently and openly, acting with integrity and honesty, keeping your focus on the business and sharing credit with your employees. This makes you the kind of boss people want to please—they want to earn your respect too—and it inspires top performance from your best people.

You can now step back from the day-to-day and evaluate yourself, your boss and your team, and you have insight that enables you to manage all of them to benefit your company and your career.

You have the tools you need to find great job candidates, make great hires, inspire them from day one, and fix or fire those who can't rise to the level your team deserves.

You know how to take input from your boss, peers and team, then make decisions confidently. You don't make mistakes often, but when you do, you have no problem admitting them to your team.

No matter where you are in your career, you will look at your situation with a clear eye and a calm head, and you will know when you need to move on. When that time comes, you will evaluate prospective bosses and teams, make good decisions about each opportunity and get the most out of every job.

Through it all, you will build a career, take care of yourself and experience joy and satisfaction far, far beyond that ever experienced by jerk managers.

But make no mistake—you are in the minority. The vast majority of your bosses and peers are not so enlightened, and you can expect them to cling to antiquated notions of management: that managers need a firm hand; that employees can't be trusted; and that working to earn your employees' respect is a sign of weakness.

None of that should affect the way you conduct yourself with your team. You must still take what you've learned here and manage your team to maximize their engagement and productivity. However, you may not want to talk about the principles in this book with your peers or bosses. Let them appreciate the results you get but don't explicitly tell them how you get them unless you are absolutely confident that they will be open to this way of thinking about management.

And know that even the best workplace has its challenges. You will have problem employees and micromanager bosses and bully peers. You will need to continue to inspire your team even as you deal with office politics, incompetence and pettiness. Your industry will change over the course of your career, and when those changes are for the worse, you may need to change industries to keep moving forward.

But by maintaining the high standards you have set for yourself and by treating your team fairly and with respect, you will triumph.

Most of all, you will become the kind of boss who inspires others to become great bosses. You can be one of the few leaders who are solving the management problems that cost US businesses hundreds of billions of dollars each year. And you will be extremely successful in the process.

www.ingramcontent.com/pod-product-compliance
Lightning Source LLC
Chambersburg PA
CBHW030635220526
45463CB00004B/1534